Best wishes

AN AUTOBIOGRAPHY

Jay Van Andel

An
Enterprising
Life

HarperBusiness
ZondervanPublishingHouse

Royalties from the sale of this book are being donated to the Van Andel Medical Research Institute.

HarperCollins books may be purchased for educational, business, or sales promotional use. For information please write: Special Markets Department, HarperCollins Publishers, Inc., 10 East 53rd Street, New York, NY 10022.

FIRST EDITION

Designed by Alma Orenstein

Insert designed by Barbara D. Knowles BDK Books Inc.

Library of Congress Cataloging-in-Publication Data

Van Andel, Jay
    An enterprising life : an autobiogrpahy / Jay Van Andel.
  — 1st ed.
      p. cm.
    Includes index.
    ISBN 0–88730–997–6
    1. Amway Corporation—History. 2. Van Andel, Jay.
    3. Businessmen—United States—Biography. I. Title.
    HF5439.H82V36 1998
    381'.13'092—dc21   98-23758

98 99 00 01 02 ❖/RRD 10 9 8 7 6 5 4 3 2 1

To Betty, my wife and dearest friend.
Her devotion and faithfulness have been the anchor
that kept me safe when the storms of life threatened.
Her living faith and everlasting love will constitute
her legacy to our children and grandchildren.

CONTENTS

ACKNOWLEDGMENTS

Capturing the memories, personal experiences, and events of seventy-three years of living, I have discovered, is no easy task.

It has been a slow, tedious, but personally rewarding endeavor. This book would never have reached the publisher's desk without the loyal and trusted support of many friends, confidants, and co-workers.

I am very much obliged to Bill Nicholson, Billy Zeoli, and Casey Wondergem, whose pleading and prodding prompted me to finally publish my life story and beliefs, and special thanks to Dr. Luis Tomatis, who encouraged me along the way.

The painstaking research efforts of poring through boxes, files, and videotape accumulated through fifty years of "stashing" was done by Sharon Sanford, and I'm grateful for her persistence.

I would be remiss if I failed to thank my four children, Nan, Steve, Barb, and Dave, for their thoughtful research interviews, which helped fill the gaps in some of my recollections.

Of great value was the mentoring and guidance of retired publisher Peter Kladder, who coached us through the complexities of producing a book. Thanks should also be extended to Lyn Cryderman, associate publisher for Zondervan, and Laureen Rowland, senior editor at HarperCollins, for their editing assistance and editorial suggestions.

I am indebted to Father Robert Sirico of the Acton Institute, whose conversations with me over the past two years helped form the outline for this book, and to other Acton staff, particularly Timothy Terrell, whose editorial assistance was invaluable to the project.

And above all I thank Almighty God for giving me the health and strength to chronicle this personal story of my passion for living, for my family, and for my faith.

FOREWORD

Rich DeVos,
Co-Founder Amway Corporation

Business partnerships of the kind I had with Jay for so many years are rare in the world of business. Many partnerships are weakened by selfishness, greed, and disloyalty, but Jay and I built our relationship on mutual respect and caring. Our business relationship had as its foundation a solid friendship and a common religious heritage. We understood each other because we had seen each other in nonbusiness surroundings. We trusted one another because both of us had been taught honesty and faithfulness by Christian parents. When we entered into various business ventures in our youth, some were successful and some weren't, but I learned Jay's strengths and weaknesses and he learned mine. By the time we started Amway in 1959, we had developed a deep-rooted respect for one another that would last a lifetime.

Since my retirement from Amway in 1992, the ties of friendship between Jay and me have remained strong. As I have confronted health problems he has been there as a help and support. My respect for Jay has increased even more as I see his generosity toward the community and the consistent, selfless help he provides his wife, Betty, through her health problems. His moral character and love for his community and family show more plainly now than ever before.

Jay's whole life has been a harmony of business skill and moral behavior. That is why this book is so important. Few people see entrepreneurship as a morally honorable endeavor. How can the businessperson in America and throughout the world reconcile the entrepreneurial vocation with his moral duties? What can the entrepreneur do to care for his neighbors, his family, and the environment?

Jay and I have always thought that the best way to expand human well-being in the present, to provide for our children, and to reduce overuse of environmental resources is to encourage free enterprise. Jay firmly believes that free enterprise is necessary for any nation to progress, and he has done much to advance the institution of free enterprise worldwide. Through this book, he reveals some of the struggles and triumphs of the entrepreneur in a nation largely unconvinced of the moral purity of the free-enterprise ideal.

Any nation that does not provide a hospitable working environment for entrepreneurs will find its growth stunted, its people languishing in a stagnant economy. Those countries that remove the shackles from entrepreneurs and allow these individuals to create wealth will find their people's well-being increasing by leaps and bounds every year. Amway distributors, in starting their own independent businesses, are no less entrepreneurial than Jay or I were when we started Amway. In some eighty countries and territories, these distributors act as ambassadors of entrepreneurship. In countries not entirely friendly to free enterprise, these people are helping to reveal the true benefits of free enterprise.

Jay has certainly exemplified the philanthropic spirit in our hometown of Grand Rapids, Michigan. By donating generously and often, Jay has made Grand Rapids a better place to live for everyone. Giving is a tradition with both of us, and we have passed down that tradition to our children. Jay's crowning achievement in philanthropy is the Van Andel Institute for Research and Education, which will bring pathbreaking medical research to western Michigan. The advances brought to medicine through Jay and Betty's support could improve the lives of millions, including those not yet born.

Any story of Jay's life must include a great deal of Amway's origin and growth into the $7 billion consumer products company it is today. But Jay's goal with this book is not to retell the story of Amway in the context of his own life. Jay's thoughts and activities have spanned so much more than Amway. He is comfortable discussing economics, politics, engineering, and business strategy, and he does so with intelligence, captivating stories, and a dry wit.

I thank God for a partner like Jay.

Paul Harvey,
ABC Radio News Commentator

For half a century I have known Jay Van Andel as such a quiet giant that I feared his thrilling, inspiring experiences would never be properly related.

At long last they have been recorded and in his own words. What a story!

Once upon a time Jay, a schoolboy, offered a classmate a ride to school every day in Jay's Model A Ford—in exchange for twenty-five cents a week gas money.

That day Jay Van Andel demonstrated his first acumen as an entrepreneur.

The classmate was Rich DeVos.

From that epic friendship Amway was born.

Jay Van Andel was a confidant of several of the world's great heads of state. He might well have been elected or appointed to any public office of his choosing.

Nobody ever loved his country more, but Jay's "choosing" was Amway.

In these pages you are going to share the legacy of his enormous reservoir of experience.

And what is more important—and most timely—you are going to learn that a good *businessman* can be a *good* businessman.

We need more reminders of that.

I t was right there in the middle of the table, but I couldn't reach it. I could picture my arm extending the short distance to the plate and then my hand grasping it up, pulling it closer so I could eat my dinner. But my body seemed sluggish, slow to respond to my wishes.

I am not a young man anymore. When I was, I teamed up with another young man and we decided to try our hand at business. After a few false starts—some successful, others not—we started a business in the basements of our homes in Ada, Michigan, just a few miles east of Grand Rapids. It worked well enough to lead the pundits at *Forbes* and *Fortune* to include us on their lists of the wealthiest people in America.

Like most success stories, mine is filled with a lot of ups and downs, and in this book I will tell you about them. I will tell you how we tried to start an airline with planes that had a tendency to run out of gas. I will tell you how we decided soap would be a better product to sell than bread. I will tell you how we created the plan that has given a better life to the three million distributors around the world who sell our product. And I will tell you the truth about our battles with the government and the press.

If you are looking for a magic bullet—a surefire gimmick that will make you a millionaire overnight—you're looking in the wrong place. In fact, you will be surprised when you learn how I got where I am today. It has a lot to do with that plate in the middle of the table.

Try as I might, I just couldn't reach it. Most days the symptoms of this frustrating condition are minor. This was not one of those days. Pretty embarrassing, especially when you've lived an active, robust life as I have. One of the universal characteristics of an entrepreneur is the ability to get things done, and over the years I've managed to help bring a lot of good things into existence. The success of our company has allowed Rich and me to build research and manufacturing facilities that stretch out over 4.2 million square feet in eighty different buildings. We've helped rebuild the downtown area of our city with a new hotel, museum, arena, aquarium, and medical facilities, and we've sponsored numerous events in the cultural and fine arts fields. I mention this not to boast but to help illustrate how frustrating it was for me not to be able to grab that plate.

Fortunately, I was dining with a close friend who, sensing my struggle and not saying a word, reached over and pushed the plate toward me. With that small act, he illustrated a profound business concept that Rich DeVos and I have practiced from the beginning: teamwork. Our company would not be where it is today without the help of others. Rich and I somehow knew we needed each other to succeed. In fact, I doubt that there would be an Amway today if either one of us had tried to create it alone. Once we got started, we learned that sharing opportunities with others who want to succeed and aren't afraid of a little hard work is the surest way to the top. We've built a $7 billion consumer products firm with the help of energetic citizens from some eighty nations and territories around the world—one of the best teams in the history of international business!

But this book is more than a history of Amway. Much has already been written about the unique success of our company and the people who have enjoyed greater financial security and personal fulfillment through it. While I will tell you a lot of stories that you've never heard before, this is really a book about ideas, the principles that allow entrepreneurial endeavors like Amway to flourish. If all you get from this book are the events of my life and the history of Amway, you will have missed the point. It is less important to me that you know what I did than why I did it.

While I am first an entrepreneur, many of my years have been spent in political activity of one sort or another (some would even say that to be a successful entrepreneur you had better pay attention to politics). I have befriended princes and presidents, suffered mightily under senseless rules and regulations, and defended lower taxes and lower tariffs. For many years I worked with the U.S. Chamber of Commerce, and for one of those years I was chairman. Believe me, Washington doesn't look any better from the inside! But it does no good to whine, which is why part of this book will unfold some of my political beliefs and how I have tried to use my wealth to support those beliefs in the political arena.

I also hope you come away from this book with a sense of how the market economy and morality fit together. The free-enterprise system and traditional morals are not at odds with one another—they're perfectly compatible, regardless of what some critics say. I am concerned about the image that successful businesses and their leaders are getting, largely from left-ward-leaning critics whose ideology gets in the way of their objectivity.

While anyone can make a case against free enterprise and capitalism based on a few isolated examples of excess and greed, the fact is that most successful businesses rely on traditional values such as integrity, honesty, and compassion, and they give back far more than they take. In fact, the spin-off effects of great fortunes are those things from which everyone is free to benefit.

Government, with its mammoth budgets, can never substitute for hardworking, beneficent individuals. No government is as in touch with a community's needs as a local citizen can be. No government has the flexibility and sensitivity to meet those needs that a wise philanthropist possesses. No government can demonstrate real faith in a city or inspire people like private generosity can. But most importantly, a philanthropist is giving away his own money, not someone else's.

Finally, I need to be up front with you about the source from which I receive my greatest help: my personal relationship with God. I realize that religion can be a controversial subject and that not everyone believes as I do. While I am not out to convert you or criticize your own beliefs, I cannot write an honest book without referring to my faith and how it has shaped every business decision I have made.

In fact, as time passes I am made more aware of the true source of my strength. We humans—especially we who are entrepreneurs—resist dependence, thinking that somehow we can find our own way, provide for ourselves, and maintain progress without God's continuing intervention in our lives. As independent and self-sufficient as I may feel when my health is good, my business is flourishing, and my family is well, all of these are blessings from God's hand. He may choose to take some of these good things away for a time to teach us how to love and trust him in our weakness, for we are always weak and vulnerable, even when we think everything is just fine. It is important to remember that because it is through our vulnerability that God is able to show us that his strength is our strength.

Upon learning about my intentions to write this book, a lot of my friends have asked about it. They wonder if it will be a history of Amway or a book about my political beliefs or an autobiography. Or will it be a "how-to" book? Or a travelogue? Or an inspirational book?

Actually, it is all of that and more because what I really wanted to do was tell a story. A story about the potential of every human who is fortunate enough to live in freedom, who is willing to work hard, who is not afraid of failure, who allows God to guide him, and who is humble enough to accept a helping hand. In a nutshell, that's the story of true success. It may not always end in material wealth, but it will always bring happiness and inner peace.

CHAPTER 1

Opportunity Beckons

I t all started with a bankruptcy.

My grandfather worked day and night to try to keep his three bike shops and a blacksmith shop afloat in the Dutch city of Haarlem. But by 1909 he reluctantly closed his businesses, not sure what he would do to provide for his family. His sister had already emigrated to Chicago, and when she heard of his plight she urged him to come to the land of opportunity. So in 1910, at the age of fifty, my grandfather, Christian, took his wife, Elizabeth, and their sons, James (my father) and Christian, to Chicago. To an entire generation of men like my grandfather, America offered a chance to make life better for their families.

Once in the United States, Christian took a job painting Pullman railroad cars in a Chicago factory. The working conditions soon gave him health problems, however, and because of this and his unfamiliarity with the English language, Christian turned to farming. My father, James, younger and more adaptable, dove into the booming automobile business. In 1921, he opened an auto dealership in Holland, Michigan, handling Gray, Chevrolet, and International vehicles. Eleven years later he joined John Flikkema, another Dutchman, and expanded to Chryslers and Plymouths. In fact, if you exit north off Interstate 96, you'll see "Van Andel and Flikkema" still selling cars on Plainfield Avenue in Grand Rapids.

Dad married Petronella ("Nellie") Van der Woude, of Holland, Michigan, and on June 3, 1924, I was born in their apartment above the Cherry Inn in Grand Rapids (which remains to this day). Most of my early childhood memories center around our home on Dickinson Street near Boston Square on the southeast side of Grand Rapids, where our family moved four years later. There were many large families with young children with whom I could play after school and every free day except part of Saturday and all day Sunday. Saturday was catechism day for children who, like me, were being brought up in the Christian Reformed Church, a fairly strict Protestant denomination tracing back to John Calvin. On Sundays there were two church services, and I had to wear church clothes throughout the day, a requirement that precluded football games and roughhousing on that holy day. Many of us CRC kids attended a neighborhood Sunday-school class taught by the very zealous Miss Goossens, where we were taught the essentials of the Reformed faith. Two basic distinctives of Reformed churches were the emphasis on the sovereignty of God and the responsibility of man to live faithfully by God's word in every part of life, and as I look back I'd have to say that all my political, economic, and entrepreneurial beliefs come from these two tenets of my religious upbringing.

We were taught that being a Christian was more than church and Sunday-school attendance. It involved the living out of biblical values of honesty, generosity, and respect for others in our everyday lives. I recall finding a dime once in a back alley near our home. A dime was quite a bit of money in those days, and so I told my mother of my discovery. She asked me to go door to door on the street to find out if anyone had lost a dime. It may sound like a silly thing to do today, but in the early 1930s many people were out of work and would miss ten cents. For my mother it was also an opportunity to teach me the importance of respecting other people's property. As it turned out, I found no one who would claim the dime, and I was allowed to keep it.

My mother and father were both devout believers, and the Van Andel household was run in accordance with high standards of morality. My father, in good Dutch tradition, considered work the duty of a Christian. He repaired and sold cars to provide for his family and to bring glory to God. We were taught that even in the way you did your job you were living out your Christian faith. The demands of running his business in a depressed economy kept him away from home much of the time, but by his example and his work he encouraged me to apply my faith to every area of my life.

From my father comes much of my personality and my business philosophy. Sometimes my father could come across as gruff or standoffish, but those who knew him well found him a caring man, dedicated to his family and his community. His relationship with Mother was a model for my relationship with my wife, Betty. Dad's love and servant's heart toward her lasted throughout their entire marriage. When, late in life, my mother was afflicted by a crippling, degenerative disease, my father demonstrated true Christian virtue by personally caring for her. Of course, I could not have known back then how deeply I would need to draw from this lesson.

Mother was of Frisian Dutch descent, and she had come from a family of nine children. Her father had gone bankrupt in the Netherlands, just as her father-in-law had, and the Van der Woude family immigrated to the United States to start over. Mr. Van der Woude became a home designer and builder, and young Nellie learned all the household skills that were taught to girls of that time. Mother was an outstanding cook. One of my favorites was "boercole," or farmer's cabbage, made of kale and potatoes, in a gravy base. It was the sort of meal to warm one's middle on bone-chilling Michigan nights.

Mother was not one to spend all of her time with cooking and housekeeping, however. She didn't hold a "job" as such, but she put her energy to good use in a thousand different ways. Mother had a car to herself, which was unusual for women in the 1930s, and that gave her the freedom to participate in all kinds of worthwhile activities outside the home. She was involved in almost every church activity and belonged to many community organizations—mostly charitable in nature. From Mother I learned the importance of involvement in the community. She regarded service to others as a central aspect of an even more important service to God.

From early childhood, at home and at school, I was taught that the only true foundation for faith and life is God's word. Today this view is unfashionable, and those who make claims to exclusive belief are ridiculed. "Tolerance" is the key word these days, but it seems to have taken on a new meaning. We are encouraged to tolerate everything, no matter how strange, except the belief that there is only one way to salvation from sin. That, and all other traditional doctrines, are not to be tolerated. What the opponents of religious faith really are advocating is a kind of intolerance: intolerance of the idea of truth and of our responsibilities before God. This is why such practices as prayer in schools, once common, are not allowed any-more. Prayer suggests a belief in certain unchanging truths.

Oakdale Christian School, on Fisk Street, was the alterna-tive to public school for children in our neighborhood. It was a good school, and many parents sacrificed even during the tight depression years to provide their children with an Oakdale education. We were taught the traditional reading, writing, and arithmetic, using the tried-and-true methods of the time. We were also taught how to swear. Mr. George Van Wesep, the principal (and Helen DeVos's father), would occasionally show classic movies to us, being careful to censor any unsavory parts by holding his hand over the projector lens. One infamous line, spoken by a British officer in a film about the War for American Independence, escaped his notice and for weeks was the source of much glee at Oakdale: "Disperse, ye damned rebels!"

In October 1929, the stock market crashed, plunging the United States into the Great Depression. I was too young to understand what had happened at the time, but several years later a local bank went under, taking my small savings account with it. Later, I got back five cents on the dollar, along with a valuable lesson about the nature of banks.

Money was scarce during the depression, so our after-school entertainment had to be cheap. In the summertime, my pals and I would explore the neighborhood, climbing coal piles at Boersma's coal yard, taking rides on the empty strap-rail carts at the Grande Brick Company, or watching auto mechan-ics, shoemakers, and backyard chicken butchers as they worked. Nearby Silver Creek was encased in a huge, blocks-long underground tunnel, which provided endless hours of adventuresome candlelit exploration. The streets, which had almost no automobile traffic, were perfect places for roller-skate hockey and ball games. Chalk marks on the new asphalt served as bases—the only disadvantage was that we couldn't make spectacular slides into home plate unless we wanted to leave some skin behind. On the rare occasions when we had ten cents, we could enjoy a well-packed ice cream cone from the East End Creamery. More accessible were the treats from Hoxie's soda fountain or Kinsel's candy store. Ice-cold pop (red, green, orange, or cola) was available for a nickel at Vern's gas station. In the fall, some of us would gather right across the street from our house and make a bonfire. We could spend hours talking, roasting marshmallows, and smoking cornsilk. During the winter, or when I tired of outdoor ramblings, I would spend hours working on model airplanes from Kuizema's hardware store.

One man in the neighborhood was in the home construction business, and some of us neighborhood kids would help him with building homes in the area. Walls in those days were built by nailing laths to the studs and then plastering over the laths. We had a lot of fun doing that and learned a lot about working hard and doing a quality job. During the summertime I and some of the other boys would make some pocket money mowing lawns.

The depression hit our family close to home when the housing industry fell into a long slump in the thirties. My maternal grandfather lost his construction business and was financially devastated. For a period of time he came to live with us, which turned out to be an extremely positive experience for me. I was able to spend a lot of time with Granddad, and the impact he had on my life is immeasurable. Can you imagine in-laws moving in with you today?

Granddad was an architect, a builder, a woodworker, and an entrepreneur while he had his construction business. As he told me about his work and demonstrated his woodworking skills, I became fascinated with the way things were designed and put together. Years later, the interest Granddad sparked led me to take courses in engineering and join the Army Air Corps.

What really set my grandfather apart was his rich faith and the way he wove his traditional theology into every aspect of his life. When Granddad lived in Holland, Michigan, I would go to visit and take walks with him around town. Very often, we would walk from 19th Street down to 9th Street, in the center of town. Granddad would take his place on a bench in the public square, where a lot of the local men had gathered to discuss theology—all in Dutch, of course. I found a spot next to Granddad and listened in as these men pleaded the merits of creationism or demonstrated the errors of Armenius, a theologian who believed God gave man the freedom to accept or reject him. (I think they're still arguing that one somewhere!) Granddad could hold his own in a debate, and he earned the respect of anyone who heard him. Years later, he told me that he had always wished he could go to a seminary to study. Granddad showed me that one's theological foundation should always be carefully considered and that true faith is lived out not just in a pew on Sundays but in every other part of life.

EXCHANGE OF A LIFETIME

If all of this helped shape my character, it was a 1929 Model A that shaped my career. In 1939 I entered Grand Rapids Christian High School. I lived all the way across town from the school, and I used to ride my bicycle several miles to school every day, until at the age of fifteen my father gave me a 1929 Model A Ford. My family was middle-class, but we always had cars to drive because my father was in the automobile business. Most high school kids weren't so blessed—I was one of only two students at Christian High School to have a car. Being the owner of a car made me pretty popular, as you might imagine. The Model A had a rumble seat, so I had extra room for passengers. Charging riders twenty-five cents a week for a ride to school was my way of paying for gas (which in those days was ten cents a gallon) and making a little extra spending money. One day a fellow named Rich DeVos approached me about a ride. He lived just a couple of blocks away from me, so of course I was happy to take his quarter every week. What would follow from that simple exchange was more than anyone could have guessed.

Rich and I gradually got to know one another, and we became good friends. We double-dated together, went to basketball games together, had fun together, and talked about what we wanted to do with our lives. Rich was more gregarious than I was, more extroverted, always making a little more noise. I was more of a bookworm, quieter than Rich, but despite our differences I enjoyed his presence—it brought out the best in me. We found in time that our different personalities perfectly complemented one another, so that the two of us made an unbeatable pair at whatever we set our minds to doing. By the time I graduated from high school in 1942, we knew that we were friends for life.

I treasure a note that Rich sent me many years later on the occasion of my thirty-ninth birthday, which shows just how constant and faithful a friend he has been through the years:

> Dear Jay:
>
> Happy Birthday! Just a note to tell you how much you have meant to me personally. Over the past 25+ years we have had our differences, but something greater has always shown through. I don't know if there is any simple way to say it, but it could be called mutual respect. A better word could be "love."
>
> The years have been good to us in so many ways that it is difficult to isolate specifics but the thrills and joys are mainly in the fact that we have done it together. It really

did begin with that 25¢ a week ride, and it's been one beautiful ride ever since.

Thanks for being what you are.

Sincerely, Rich

Some people are accused of buying their friends, but I guess you could say I did just the opposite. Two other friends who rode in that rumble seat and became very dear to me in high school were Marv Van Dellen and John Vanderveen. We would often go fishing or skiing together, and with Rich, we formed a foursome that lasted through high school, wartime, marriage, careers, and even to the present day.

It wasn't long before I began working for my dad, enlisting Rich's help now and then. When I was sixteen years old, and Rich was fourteen, Dad asked us to help him by delivering two used pickup trucks to a customer in Bozeman, Montana. Of course, we jumped at the chance. Today, of course, no caring parent would ask such a thing, but the United States of 1940 was a safer place. To us, a more exciting adventure was not imaginable. We thought of ourselves out in the broad open spaces of the West, meeting the various challenges of the road with our own strength and abilities. The prospect appealed to our deeply ingrained sense of self-reliance and independence. As the first of the many adventures that Rich and I were to embark upon over the course of our lives, the teamwork and companionship that we built on that trip were to serve us well in future years.

We had to be quite careful with our finances on the trip. In the summer of 1940, the effects of the Great Depression lingered on, so we did everything possible to make each penny count. To avoid motel costs we slept on hay in the back of the trucks. We didn't mind at all—it was an Adventure, we were men, and we could take it. One hot day we had three flat tires at once (the truck tires had been nearly bald when we left) and we pulled to a stop in front of a service station out in the middle of nowhere. We patched the tires using the kit we had brought along and then found that the fellow in the service station wanted to charge us a nickel for air. We couldn't afford to spend our money on air, not even a nickel, so we got out our little hand pump and spent the next hour or so pumping up those three tires. I think he believed we would give in and pay him the nickel, but he didn't count on our determination and willingness to work.

WARTIME LESSONS

When I graduated from high school, the world was at war. The Movietone News at theaters showed film clips of helmeted German soldiers and powerful tanks advancing through Europe and of American troops boarding ships for the war zones. Updates on the war were on every radio. American factories were manufacturing tanks, fighter aircraft, guns, and ammunition. Ration cards were in every purse, and signs advertising war bonds were in most storefront windows. Many of my friends who graduated with me that spring were bound for military training and then service in Europe or the Pacific. I entered the Army Air Reserve Corps at Calvin College, thinking that I could choose my branch of service and perhaps finish college before turning to active service. An army captain came to the school and told us that if we signed up for reserve service immediately, we would be allowed to finish and be given a shot at Officer Training School. Not being very well schooled in life at that time, I believed him. So in November of 1942 I enlisted as a private. The following March they loaded us all on a train for the St. Petersburg, Florida, training camp. On the way down, while eating breakfast, my tray started to slide across the table, which was my first indication that the train had derailed. No one in my car was seriously hurt, but it was a rude shock to all of us.

When we finally made it to St. Petersburg, we were bar-racked in tents on what had been the golf course of a ritzy country club. The camp facilities had been slapped together without much care or common sense, and conditions were pretty bad. The open-air mess hall was right next to the slit latrines, there was no hot water, and good medical care was hard to come by—I suppose most of the doctors were being shipped overseas to the battle areas. All of us were being shot full of vaccinations, but it didn't seem to help matters because many of us got sick anyway.

At least five hundred of the men in that camp developed serious illnesses. I was one of them. The army took over a large hotel in St. Petersburg and filled it with sick GIs. I was in this makeshift hospital for a month. At first the doctors diagnosed us as having measles. I knew I didn't have measles. Measles doesn't produce severe headaches, and almost all of us were having excruciating head pain. After some of the men started dying the doctors decided it was spinal meningitis. In 1943 there was no effective cure for the disease. Doctors experi-mented with some strange things before coming up with sulfa drugs, which proved to be fairly effective.

In the meantime local citizens had complained to their con-gressmen about the Florida training camp conditions. It didn't make any sense to them, or to me, that the army should be tak-ing in thousands of men in good physical condition and send-ing half of them back home sick or crippled after a month or two in the basic training camps. Many men who did not die from disease were left permanently disabled. Some were unable to walk, some couldn't speak, and some would be plagued with chronic illness the rest of their lives. I credit the fervent prayers of many people in Grand Rapids with my eventual full recovery.

The whole experience gave me an aversion to most modern medical care. To this day, my army training camp illness has been the only time I have been admitted to a hospital. I've long been interested in alternative methods of healing and disease prevention. Of course, conventional medicine seems to work much of the time, but there is so much about the human body that we do not know—so much remaining to be discovered. Conventional theories need to be challenged, so that new ideas can be allowed to work. Dr. Ignaz Semmelweis, an obstetrician in 1840s Vienna, defied the medical reasoning of his day by insisting that medical personnel wash their hands in a sterilizing solution between patients. He saved untold thousands of human lives as a result of his persistent efforts but died before medical science accepted his results.

When I finally finished basic training, I went to bombsight school at Lowry Field in Denver, Colorado. There, I learned about the sophisticated, top-secret Norden bombsights that would help make the daytime raids over Europe and Japan so devastating. After that came aviation cadet training at Seymour Johnson Field in North Carolina. From there I went on to Yale University for Aircraft Armament Officers' School. My year there changed my whole attitude on life. The course of study was extremely rigorous, and the schedule intense. They weren't going to let any of us off easy just because officers were desperately needed for the war effort. I found myself working harder than I ever thought I could. The only place to study after lights-out at 9:00 p.m. was the shower rooms, and I found myself there some nights until reveille at 5:00 a.m. There were many times when I didn't think I would make it through, but by persistent effort I discovered I could keep up with my fellow students and even excel.

I still distinctly recall the succinct, hard-hitting speech one general made at our graduation ceremony:

Gentlemen, you are now going off to war. In war there is no excuse for failure. You cannot say that you could not predict the weather and therefore lost the battle. Or that you could not get delivery of your ammunition or that your airplanes were not delivered on time. You have to take all that into account beforehand. You win the battle anyway. If you lose the battle, you may lose the war. You will then have nothing to come home to. The enemy will take over your homeland. In war there is no excuse for failure.

After receiving my commission as a second lieutenant, the Army Air Corps put me to work training crews for the B–17 and later, B–29 bombers that reached to the Japanese mainland. Rich, meanwhile, had enlisted in the army as well and was stationed with a glider unit on the island of Tinian, in the Pacific. We kept up with each other through letters, and once or twice we were able to arrange to be stateside at the same time.

We met back in Grand Rapids, and one night when we had returned from taking a couple of girls out, Rich pulled the car into the garage at his parents' house, and we got to talking. Rich said, "Well, Jay, when this is all over, what are we going to do? Go back to college?" Both of us knew that wasn't what we really wanted to do. The more we talked, the more we realized that we ought to form a partnership and go into business together. As would happen so many times in the future, all we needed to do was figure out what kind of business we would start.

I think you'll be surprised to learn how the first Van Andel and DeVos team took off.

Getting off the Ground

Except for a few slight problems with the first business Rich and I formed, Amway today might have been an airline.

After World War II there was a kind of airplane craze. Many people thought every new house would be built near an airstrip and that there would be two airplanes in every garage so we could all commute to work by air. Since we both liked airplanes, we decided to build a business around them. Our friend Jim Bosscher proposed that the three of us pool our resources, buy an airplane, and get in on the action.

Rich was still in the army, so he sent me his share of the money so that Jim and I could start looking for an airplane. We bought a two-seat Piper Cub in Detroit for a down payment of $700. We didn't know the first thing about flying, so we had to hire a pilot to fly it from Detroit to Grand Rapids. In this way Rich became part owner of an airplane before he ever owned a car! The next difficulty was making enough money to pay off and fly the airplane we just bought.

The solution to that problem was to open a flying service. We named it Wolverine Air Service, which wasn't too original in the Wolverine State, but we didn't care. Flying instruction was our mainstay, but we also offered passenger rides, group transportation, and sales and rentals of airplanes. We still didn't know how to fly, so we hired two veteran pilots to do that job while we did the legwork on the ground. Our first instructors were Jack Baas, a former P-38 pilot, and Edward Mersman, a former B-17 pilot. Jim, who had been an airplane mechanic in the Army Air Corps during the war, handled the mechanical work.

We were counting on being able to use the new Grand River Air Park in Comstock Park, which was under construction when we started. When the airport project ran out of money, we attached pontoons to the bottom of our airplane and used the Grand River for our airstrip. This was a lesson to us in improvisation, and we learned a few more like it during our air service days. Rich loves to tell the story of how we employed the services of an old chicken coop for an office. (I still insist that it was a tool shed, but Rich's version does make a better story.)

After about a year, Jim sold out to Rich and me so that he could go back to school. Rich and I continued to run the air service during the daylight hours, but had a lot of free time during the evenings. While on a trip to Florida to deliver a plane, the idea occurred to us to open a drive-in restaurant, like ones we had seen elsewhere. We had $300 to invest, so on May 20, 1947, we opened the "Riverside Drive-Inn Restaurant," which was the very first of its kind in the area. We knew just about as much about running a restaurant as we had known about flying when we started, but we didn't let that stop us. Rich and I built a diminutive wooden structure there at the air park, laying the foundation and nailing the clapboards ourselves. It took several months to get electricity hooked up properly, so we bought a generator. We also had no water for some time, so every evening we would fill up jugs at the nearest place that had plumbing and carry them to the restaurant.

From five o'clock in the afternoon until midnight we kept the restaurant open. Rich and I traded off jobs—one night he would burn the hamburgers while I served customers, and the next night I would burn the hamburgers while he served customers.

A good entrepreneur never rests, so we were always trying to think of something else that we could provide the customers at the air park. At one point, we started offering canoe rides down the Grand River. This was a big hit, especially when we put newfangled transistor radios in the canoes for a musically accompanied tour. By arrangement with charter boat owners on Lake Superior, we also began offering fishing excursions on that lake. After just two years in business, we were operating a flight school, charter service, repair service, and aircraft and gasoline sales organization, as well as the boat rental and charter business, and the restaurant. With twelve airplanes and fifteen pilots, Wolverine Air Service was one of the leading flying services in the state of Michigan.

We learned a lot of lessons about business during these several years. We learned the value of hard work, of persistence, and of improvisation. Lesson number one was that running a business is a matter of pressing on in spite of an unending series of unexpected problems. We sometimes had trouble with airplanes running out of gas—one summer, students landed the planes in fields twenty-five times. I shudder when I think of some of the creative ways we dealt with such inconveniences.

One day, Jack Baas was piloting one of the seaplanes when it ran out of gas due to strong head winds. Forced to land in a lake too small for a normal takeoff, we wondered how we would get the plane back in the air. We bought five gallons of gas, fueled the seaplane, and tied the tail to a tree. Jack climbed in the cockpit, revved up the engine, and had me cut the plane loose with a knife at his signal. Sure enough, he made it into the air, just clearing the trees on the opposite shore.

The problems we ran into were never ending, but we persisted. When the air park didn't open on time, when the electricity and water weren't hooked up for our restaurant on time, when several of our airplane engines were destroyed after we used the wrong lubricating oil, when hail and wind seriously damaged several of our airplanes, we didn't give up. Winter snows forced us to put skis on all the airplanes, but it seemed that as soon as the skis were on, the snow would melt, and as soon as we removed them, the snow would fly. But the first year, we flew two million passenger miles and earned $50,000.

"Nothing in the world can take the place of persistence," a wise man once said. "Talent will not; nothing is more common than unsuccessful men with talent. Genius will not; unrewarded genius is almost a proverb. Education alone will not; the world is full of educated derelicts. Persistence and determination alone are omnipotent."

The second important lesson we learned from our first business was to stay out of the shop and let other people do what they do best. Delegating responsibility is essential—even for some of the most important work. When Rich and I entered the air service business, neither of us were licensed instructors. We had to hire others to do that work. This made us far more successful than the four other flying services in the region, because we were on the ground recruiting new flying students and charter customers while our competitors, who did their own instructing, were in the air. My father's garage became successful for the same reason. He had a garage but never spent his time repairing cars himself. He was always out front, talking to customers and soliciting more business.

Many business owners ignore this principle and suffer for it. They spend their time doing things that they can get others to do for them and don't spend time getting customers, which is the most important part of the business. Amway distributors can fall into this trap—they get distracted with the details of bookkeeping and shelf and warehouse details and don't spend the necessary time getting new customers. Sometimes this is because of a lack of knowledge, but sometimes it's because the business owner lacks discipline or doesn't want to spend time meeting customers. Some feel that they need to micromanage every aspect of the business, which results in frustrated employees, poorly served customers, and ultimately a dead business.

Lesson number three in our business education was to work hard, and work smart, when everyone else is asleep or watching TV. Working from nine to five provides an average standard of living. It's the work done from five to midnight that really moves you ahead in life. Rich and I worked hard at building our air service. For a while, we were both taking business classes at nearby Calvin College, so we would switch off managing the business and going to class. We had only one car between us, so I would drop Rich off at the airport at sunup and then go on to school. When my classes ended at noon, I would run to the car, race out to the airport, and Rich would take the car and try to make it back to campus for his twelve-twenty class. When Rich finished, he would drive back out to the airport and go back to work. This went on for about a year. Eventually, both of us decided that we should devote all of our time to developing the business, and we dropped out.

We really had to rush around to get everything done, especially after we started the restaurant. Often we would work until the wee hours of the morning and then drive over to Lake Michigan to swim, relax, and catch forty winks on the beach before rising early for another day of managing the business. We were exhausted, but the work was fulfilling.

WORK AS AN ETHIC

Day in and day out, Rich and I worked at building our airplane business and the restaurant. Even though it physically exhausted us, we knew we were doing the right thing by putting all we had into the business, by striving to make every day count. Our Christian upbringing taught us that work is a good thing. It is difficult, to be sure, but it is part of what God put us here on this planet to do.

From my Calvinist heritage, I learned that our work is done in the context of a calling, which assures us that, no matter what our income level, education, or family background, we each are equal in our ability to glorify God in our work. In following our calling, John Calvin writes, "No work will be so mean and sordid as not to have a splendor and value in the eye of God." Even though people around us may not recognize or give honor to our work, God is pleased if we do our work for his glory.

Because work is not an end in itself, we have to work intelligently to make sure that what we do produces something of value—something useful or attractive. One of the best ways to know whether the fruit of our labor has value is to try to sell it in the marketplace. If our work has no value to other human beings, it will not sell. If we are rational people, and most of us are, then we will change our work to produce something that other people want. This is what the system of free enterprise encourages.

Ethical considerations enter into this, of course. Moral people should not produce things that clearly bring dishonor to

God, even if people express a desire for such things. In my opinion, it is immoral to be involved in the production of pornography, the provision of abortions, prostitution, or even the production of literature or media ventures that undermine the family. It's for this reason that I believe free enterprise works best when guided by traditional Judeo-Christian principles.

Within the realm of legitimate business activity, however, the prices dictated by the market are a wonderful, natural way to provide for society's needs. The decisions of the entrepreneur involve how best to provide the consumer with what he wants. Each entrepreneur competes with other entrepreneurs to provide the service better, faster, and with a pleasant attitude toward the customer. There is nothing immoral about profits—profits are a reward for serving the customer well. Profits are also the source of capital for all business. A business with no profit will eventually fail for lack of money to grow or replace facilities. To be a good entrepreneur means to put others' needs ahead of your own: It is to be a good servant. And if you do it well enough, you will be rewarded for your work.

Of course, Rich and I didn't have a lot of time to think through these concepts while we were trying to build our business. Fortunately, they were woven into the very fabric of our souls, thanks to godly parents and years of going to church and Sunday school.

CHAPTER 3

Having Fun

After three successful years of building our aircraft business, Rich and I decided to take a year off and have some fun. The GI Bill that had funded many of our studies was about to run out, and we just weren't ready to settle down yet. We needed another big adventure while we were still young. In the winter of 1948, we both read the book *Caribbean Cruise*, by the yachtsman Richard Bertram, and the thought of a sailing adventure appealed to us in the same way that the trip to Montana did when we were eight years younger. We were fond of being out on our own, with nothing to restrain us. The vacations we had taken the year before, to Mexico and Key West by air, were not entirely satisfying because we had to leave after only a few days to tend to our rapidly growing business. Now, we would be free to take our time, act on a whim if it so pleased us, and see what awaited us in the warm Caribbean.

We went to South Norwalk, Connecticut, and looked over a thirty-eight-foot schooner named *Elizabeth*. She was a pre-war wooden boat, ten years old, and had spent the war sitting in dry dock. We were pretty ignorant of marine matters at the time and didn't realize that this would cause the hull to dry out and leak. At the time, we thought *Elizabeth* would be perfect for the kind of trip we would be taking, so we sold one of our airplanes and bought the boat.

FROM THE DEPTHS

Neither of us had ever had a tiller in his hand before, so Rich hired a captain and one crew member to help us get started. While I went back to Michigan to close out the airplane business, Rich sailed south to Wilmington, North Carolina. Unfortunately, Rich wasn't a quick study at navigation, and while the captain was asleep one night, he made a slight detour into a New Jersey swamp. "Nobody's ever been this far inland in a boat this size before," an amazed Coast Guard sailor told them as he hauled the *Elizabeth* out at the end of a rope. He towed them out into Delaware Bay and said, "That's the ocean, boys. Turn that little compass south and follow it until you get warm, then turn right and you'll be in Florida."

Rich left the *Elizabeth* in Wilmington and joined me in Grand Rapids for Christmas. Early in January we returned to North Carolina, and on January 17, 1949, we left the captain and crewman behind and set sail for Miami. There we would outfit the boat for the Caribbean.

Learning to sail a boat, we discovered, was a lot like starting a business. We didn't know any more about sailing than we did about flying airplanes when we launched the airplane business, but we jumped in anyway. We made a lot of mistakes, but we kept plugging away, and every day we learned something new.

We had made some vague plans to sail south to Cuba, then to the Dominican Republic, Puerto Rico, Venezuela, and around the Atlantic side of the South American continent. Rich and I noticed on the way down to Florida that the *Elizabeth* was a leaker. The bilge pumps were keeping up well enough, however, so we thought little of it and kept going. After a stop in Miami, we sailed to Key West, then across the Straits of Florida to Havana and finally to the Cuban town of Caibarién, where we had the seams recaulked by some local fishermen.

We left Caibarién about the third week in March. The next leg of our trip was a long beat into the wind along the north coast of Cuba toward Haiti. The weather was fairly nice, though it was a head sea and a little rough. About six o'clock on the evening of the 27th Rich checked below and noticed some water coming in. He turned the bilge pumps on and came back up topside where I was sleeping. Half an hour later he went below again and the water was deeper, so he woke me up and we started pumping by hand. We had one crewman with us by this time, a Cuban named Lazaro Hernandez, but, being ill with an infected tooth, he was little help. The water was coming in faster than we could pump it out, so we cranked the engine and used the hose from the cooling intake to suck water out of the bilges. It soon became apparent that this was not going to work either.

By this time, we were very concerned. We were about ten miles offshore at this time, and eighty-five miles from the nearest port. We saw a lighthouse on the Bahamas side of the channel and tried all sorts of sail combinations to try to make it there, but we eventually had to turn back toward the coast of Cuba. We realized then that we were in real trouble, and we sent out an SOS on our radio.

Fortunately we were in a major shipping lane, off the Paridon Grande anchorage in the Bahama Channel, so every few hours a ship would come by. Around midnight a ship's lights appeared and we sent up a red flare. The ship answered the distress sign and signaled us in Morse code, but we didn't know Morse, so we just replied with an SOS on our searchlight. Apparently that didn't satisfy the captain, for when the ship had come within about half a mile of us, it abruptly turned about. Probably he thought we were grounded on rocks and didn't want to put a hole in his freighter trying to rescue us. Two or three hours later we sighted another ship, which came alongside, and not a bit too soon, either, because at 2:30 A.M. a plank in the bow broke loose and water started pouring in.

The ship, I remember, was the *Adabelle Lykes,* a freighter bound for Puerto Rico. The captain leaned over the gunwale and shouted down to us, "Who are you?"

"The schooner *Elizabeth,* out of Michigan," Rich said.

"What in hell are you doing down here?" said the captain.

"Sinking!" Rich replied.

The crew of the *Adabelle* tried to hoist our vessel out of the water and onto the deck with one of their cargo booms, but this proved impossible—our sailboat was too full of water. We were given ten minutes to gather together whatever we could off the *Elizabeth,* and we were able to salvage most of our clothes, money, and personal items. Then the captain, a Mr. W. H. Files, allowed his crew to board our boat and strip it of whatever they could before he sank it. Those men were able to strip more things off that boat than I ever realized were there. I was a little embarrassed that I had allowed so much to escape my notice.

The last man on board chopped a large hole in the hull and scrambled up the rope ladder to the freighter's deck. Then the captain backed off several hundred yards, put on speed, and smashed into the *Elizabeth,* breaking it up. The boat scraped along the side of the *Adabelle Lykes,* sinking fast. By the time it reached the stern of the ship, the tip of the mast had vanished beneath the waves. This was necessary to keep the *Elizabeth* from becoming a floating hazard to other shipping, but it was still a very sad moment for Rich and me. I don't think our vessel, buoyant as it was, would have actually sunk under us if the *Adabelle* hadn't come along, but it is nevertheless an extremely uncomfortable feeling to be in a swamped boat at night, ten miles from shore in 1,500 feet of water, where there is a real risk of being run over by the next freighter that comes along.

Rich and I didn't know much about maritime life when we departed on our journey, but we knew enough about risks to take out an insurance policy on the *Elizabeth*. We filed a claim on the boat when we reached Puerto Rico and sent most of our stuff for safekeeping to Fred Morgan, a friend of Rich's in New Orleans. Rich and I didn't see any point in cutting short our trip just because our boat sank from under us, so we decided to continue on to South America.

We boarded the British tramp tanker *Teakwood,* bound for Caracas, Venezuela. The captain was not allowed to take on passengers, so he paid us a shilling each and took us on as crewmen. He was pretty glad to have us, too, because his whole English crew had quit, leaving him with an entirely Puerto Rican replacement crew. He was so glad to have someone on board who spoke English that, after we reached our destination, he encouraged us to continue on to Africa with him. The food and water were pretty bad, however, so we declined and chose to disembark at Willemstad, Curaçao.

We had to literally jump ship when we arrived at Curaçao. The immigration officials at Willemstad wouldn't allow crewmen to leave the ship, because people would often try to immigrate illegally that way. Curaçao is a Dutch territory, so I started explaining our situation to the immigration people in their native Dutch. This really set them off, because they were sure that "no one in the United States speaks Dutch," and so we must be communist spies. They demanded that we show that we had the means to get a ticket out of Curaçao, so we showed the official the thousands of dollars we had in our money belts. This only confirmed his suspicions—we were communists who were there to foment an insurrection and raise havoc. However, they let us off the ship after taking our passports, and we went to a hotel. We did notice that we were followed there, and everywhere we went for the next three or four days, until the Curaçan government got confirmation of our identities from the U.S. government.

COLOMBIA BY STERN-WHEELER

The Curaçan officials must have been relieved when we finally left. I'm not sure we ever convinced some of them, but we did understand them a lot better when we reached Colombia. From Willemstad we flew to Caracas, Venezuela. We didn't stay long in Venezuela because the rate of exchange wasn't in our favor, so we flew east to Barranquilla, Colombia. Barranquilla is located at the mouth of the Magdalena River, a major watercourse that drains the more densely populated Colombian interior. Rich and I discovered an old stern-wheeler, just like the ones that used to ply the Mississippi—in fact, this one had been transported from the Mississippi for use on the Magdalena. This boat and others like it were the main means of transportation on the Magdalena. It served triple duty as a freighter, a passenger liner, and a military transport. As there were no good roads at that time in the interior of Colombia, if we wanted to see the country, this was the only way to do it. We boarded and for $15 got a first-class cabin, which I suppose was "first class" by 1949 Colombian standards but was unimpressive to me. The alternative, however, was sleeping belowdecks in the steerage on a mat.

On the foredeck of the boat was a small herd of cattle, which diminished in number by one every day as they were slaughtered to feed the passengers. Rich and I decided that the butcher was probably an amateur after I discovered a piece of meat in my soup that still had skin and hair on it. We lost some weight on that trip! We learned to look for food whenever we had a chance to disembark, to supplement the terrible fare on board. At one stop along the river we found pineapples for five cents each, so we picked up as many as we could carry and stashed them away in our cabin.

While the boat was under way we would sit in deck chairs reading or watching the green jungle unfold around the bends of the river. One day as Rich and I were dozing in the sun, we woke to the sound of anxious shouting and carrying-on from the opposite side of the boat. We rushed around the stern just in time to see one of the passengers slip by in the brown water, frantically waving his arms and shouting something in Spanish. A small knot of people was rushing toward us along the gun-wale, uselessly shouting at the poor fellow. Two thrown life preservers failed to reach him before the swift current swept him far astern. The captain appeared and a heated argument ensued. The captain, it seemed, was not going to put the entire boat at risk turning about in the fast-moving current and narrow channel, so the man was left to fend for himself. It is likely that he drowned. Rich and I decided that day that we didn't want to fall overboard.

At night there was no way to safely navigate the river, so the captain would pull the bow of the stern-wheeler into the riverbank, throw an anchor off the stern, and stay put for the night. Nighttime in the jungle was very unlike anything I had experienced in my life. The noises are so very different. On a sailboat, when night falls one can hear the slap of water against the side, the creaking and popping of the wooden planks in the hull, the stretching and straining of the anchor ropes, and, on a leaker like the *Elizabeth,* the noise of the bilge pumps. At night in the jungle on a crowded riverboat, there are so many more sounds. Besides the "people noises" from the deck below us, there were distant machinery noises from the steam engine and the measured step of one of the booted guards patrolling the deck. Our cabin got stuffy at night, so we would walk out on the deck and listen to the squawkings, screechings, and howlings of whatever creatures lived a hundred yards into the jungle. Only a few of them actually made it onto the boat, those being mostly of the insect variety. There were June beetles everywhere. Thousands of them would land on the deck, attracted by the boat lights, and they would crunch under our shoes as we walked about.

The Colombia we saw was being torn apart before our eyes. In 1949 Colombia was into the second year of "La Violencia," a bloody conflict that lasted for a decade and claimed the lives of two hundred thousand Colombians. There was a lot of anti-American sentiment in the country at that time—we noticed signs saying "Yankees Go Home" and the like. Communism was gaining favor with many Colombians, and we didn't feel entirely at ease carrying our U.S. passports around. As there were bandits in the area who would try to hold up the riverboats at night and rob the passengers, Colombian troops would stand guard on the shore at night. This should have made us feel more comfortable, I suppose, but somehow their presence just reminded us of the danger.

We Americans seem to have a habit of making enemies in foreign countries. While American culture is embraced all over the world (sometimes to our well-deserved embarrassment), the political or military influence we wield in many nations is often resented by local citizens. American troops are sent overseas to protect what Washington politicians see as our best interests, but if an American military presence incites people against us, the effect may be to shoot ourselves in the foot. At enormous cost to ourselves through higher defense expenditures, we reduce the success of American exporters and manufacturers in foreign markets. But politicians don't seem to understand the power of American business to peacefully gain the cooperation of foreign nations. Because people worldwide like American products, American businessmen make much more effective ambassadors than American troops.

IN THE UNDERGROUND

Of course, Rich and I were on a vacation, and such things didn't occupy our minds for long. We continued steaming along the Magdalena River until it became too shallow for navigation and disembarked at a little town that had a train to Medellín. Medellín is better known today for the drug trade that originates in that area, but in 1949 we made no such connection. The city is nestled in a high, forested valley in the Andes Mountains. The altitude contributed to a refreshing cool climate, which we greatly appreciated after our time in the tropical heat. From Medellín we took a plane to Cali, and from Cali we boarded a narrow-gauge Aeros-Euro train for Buenaventura. The little train was almost like a child's toy railroad. The passenger cars had open sides, which we didn't think would matter much until we went through a tunnel. Rich and I burst out laughing at each other when we emerged—we looked like coal miners at quitting time. The soot from the steam locomotive, having no place to go in the tunnel, wound up on our faces and hands.

At Buenaventura I had to negotiate on the black market to get money for tickets on the next leg of our journey—a Grace liner down the west coast of South America. This was one of my first experiences with an underground economy, and it piqued my interest. In most respects, currency is just like any other good. Currency has a "price" just like anything else, only we have to express that price in terms of other currencies, which we call the exchange rate. Worldwide, almost without exception, the production of currency is completely controlled by the government. The government usually takes the opportunity presented by its money monopoly to inflate the currency and thereby extract value to use for its own purposes. If a government outrageously and persistently debases the currency, people flee to other currencies in an attempt to preserve the value of their monetary assets. Of course, government officials know that they can't inflate the currency at their usual rate if people can just switch to another currency. So the officials try to stop people from doing this by setting an artificially high exchange rate—in other words, a high "price" on foreign currencies in terms of the domestic currency. This kind of law is extremely difficult to enforce, however, so a black market in foreign currency quickly forms.

Though our general plan was to circle the continent of South America, we never were quite sure where we would go next. Part of the adventure was never buying tickets beyond the next destination. Rich and I took South America as it came to us, not confining ourselves to detailed itineraries.

PLANNING FOR FREEDOM

We couldn't leave behind our entrepreneurial "natures," though. Everywhere we went, we kept our eyes open to opportunities to import items into the United States. Rich and I spent much of our time talking at length about what we would do when we returned to the States. There was no question in our minds that we would start some kind of business again. We weren't sure what it would be, but we had proven to ourselves that we could succeed together.

The Grace liner we boarded in Buenaventura was a combination freight boat and passenger liner. We made many stops along the way, in Ecuador, Peru, and Chile, as the boat would off-load bananas and pick up sugarcane or cotton. We got off for good in Valparaiso, which is the harbor town for Santiago,

Chile. We were so tired of traveling by this time that we decided to stay a while in Santiago. Exploring the countryside, riding horses, and going to parties took about a month of our time. I have some facility in languages, so I was able to learn just enough Spanish to get myself in trouble.

Chile has a dry Mediterranean-like climate similar to California's. We were there in the winter season, so it was a little cool. Santiago was then, and still is, one of the most developed, cosmopolitan cities in South America. It had a very international flavor to it, as thousands of resident Europeans were there. Just sitting in one of the many fine restaurants in Santiago will give the traveler a taste of the city. I remember one day Rich and I carried on a conversation in a restaurant there in English, Spanish, and Dutch. Neither one of us had very good Spanish, but the locals were very friendly and patient with us. Santiago and its people were so delightful that we decided to spend a few weeks there.

After a month in Santiago, we flew to what would be the southern terminus of our South American tour, Buenos Aires. Argentina is known for its beef production, and I recall that the restaurant fare there was largely beef. They even had beef blood cocktails, which I sampled in an effort to more fully experience the local culture. Halfway through the beverage I decided to stick with more traditional refreshments. Buenos Aires was as beautiful as Santiago, but the political climate cast a dark shadow over all the city's niceties.

Argentina is a sad example of a wonderful nation with beautiful people and abundant resources, repeatedly driven to its knees by socialism. At the time we were in Buenos Aires, Argentina was under the dictatorship of the socialist Juan Perón. Argentina in 1949 was a police state. There seemed to be armed men everywhere, and the rampant nationalism explained the Argentinean flags fluttering from balconies and rooftops. Once we saw Perón himself pontificating from the balcony of his streetside palace. It was reminiscent of the wartime news clips we had seen of Benito Mussolini performing from a similar balcony in Rome.

Perón retained power for eleven years despite his suppression of basic civil liberties, his betrayal of Argentine Roman Catholics, and his foolish "peronismo," or economic policies. After we left Argentina, the country went into a protracted economic decline brought about by peronismo. To satisfy farmers and labor unions in Argentina, Perón had resorted to price-fixing and protectionist measures. As a result, Argentina lost its competitive edge. Argentina, well known as the home of the gauchos, went from being a net exporter of beef to being a net importer of beef as a result of peronismo. Severe inflation haunted the economy for decades thereafter. Perón's wife Eva, as it turned out, was actually more popular with Argentineans; when she died in 1952 of cancer, tolerance for his regime fell dramatically. He was exiled in 1955, to return several years before his death in 1974. Interestingly, the current president of Argentina, an avowed Perónist, is known for his rather un-Perón-like policies. Since taking office in 1989, Carlos Menem has stopped hyperinflation, privatized most government-owned operations, challenged labor unions, and reduced government regulation of the economy.

We finally left Juan Perón's Argentina for Uruguay and Brazil, flying first to Montevideo and then to Rio de Janeiro. There, on the beach at Copacabana, we coined the name Ja-Ri (pronounced jah-ree), for Jay and Rich, that would be the name of our business when we returned to the United States. We still weren't sure what that business would be, but we were thinking about importing at the time.

From Rio we went to Belém, a major Brazilian port near the mouth of the Amazon River. From Belém we flew to the Guyanas, completing our circle of South America. We flew from there to Trinidad, then Antigua, then to Haiti and the

Dominican Republic. In Haiti we finally hit on something we thought we could import successfully. There was a wholesaler who had a little factory, actually a string of huts, where some men and women sat carving dishes and other household items from mahogany. Rich and I decided that this was just the thing that the people back home would snatch up, so we made arrangements with the fellow and departed for Mayagüez, Cuba. When we finally flew into Miami in July 1949, we were about ready to see the United States again. We had been gone about six months, and we figured that the travel bug wouldn't hit us again for quite a while. The soil of every country in South America had been under our feet, save Bolivia and Paraguay, and that of a good many other nations in the Caribbean. We took this trip basically to have some fun, but it had a lasting effect on us.

Seeing the way people live in countries where the government controls so much taught us the importance of a free economy, and we never again took for granted the relative freedom of U.S. society. South America is an amazing continent. It is filled with vast mineral wealth, millions of acres of arable land, and environmental treasures of incalculable value. Yet in many of the countries on that continent, large numbers of people live in poverty. Why? Because for many years, governments in South America have not given their people the freedom to reach their potential. Rejection of the principle of "equality before the law" and heavy taxation have virtually eliminated the middle class in many South American countries. A tradition of corrupt, bureaucratic government and the oppressive burden of government regulation in some of the nations have stifled economic growth and kept millions in poverty. And finally, heavy government indebtedness to other nations has put many economies on a shaky footing.

Thankfully, conditions are improving and South America is emerging as a vibrant economic power. But when we were there, it was so disheartening to see so many talented and bright people locked out of a chance to succeed.

We left this beautiful continent eager to try our hand at business once again, but in an environment that rewards initiative. The only question: What kind of business would we start?

CHAPTER 4

The Nutrilite Way

I t would probably make a better story to report that Rich and I discovered a magic plant in the Amazon that became the basis for Amway's cleaning products. Well, the plant we "discovered" in the Caribbean was a fairly common tree, and it didn't exactly lead to Amway. At least not directly.

As soon as Rich and I returned from South America, we jointly formed the Ja-Ri Corporation and began importing Haitian mahogany wooden ware. We honed our sales skills on department-store purchasing agents and gift shop owners, quickly rediscovering that traveling was much easier than earning a living. The competition was tough, and we were young and inexperienced at this sort of business. Still, the importing business got off the ground and gave Ja-Ri its first profits.

I think there is something in the inner being of entrepreneurs that makes them want to be their own bosses. That has been true of me, at least. My mother used to tell me that when I was very small, I sometimes resisted when she began to help me with small tasks. "Me do it" became my motto for early childhood, and ever since I've had a desire to do my own thing.

After starting the importing business, Rich and I didn't hesitate to start other enterprises we thought might turn a profit. For a while we ran ice cream carts in the Grand Rapids area, then we went in with a friend of ours named Peter Price to start a toy company. Grand Rapids Toy Company began with the manufacture and distribution of a wooden rocking horse on which we held patents. Rich was president, our friend Peter was the vice president, and I was the secretary and treasurer. The company was, in short, a disaster. The high-quality, expensive toys we were trying to sell just weren't what consumers wanted at that time. The Grand Rapids Toy Company was one of our entrepreneurial endeavors that bit the dust early and hard. It was an expensive lesson in how not to do it. We wound up the venture by buying back the stock of our stockholders at the price they paid for it, so they suffered no losses.

Another venture was the Stone Mill Products Company, a wholesale and retail baked-goods business. Before "organic" was trendy, we were going door to door selling natural organically grown bread and other baked goods. Some of the products we sold through mail order, which taught us that a scattered market could be well served by an organized central manufacturing facility. Stone Mill Products was a moderate success, and we sold it in 1955.

In retrospect, all these businesses that Rich and I started after we returned from South America were teaching us things about business that we would use later with Amway. The combination of experience with the flying service and the early Ja-Ri businesses prepared us to make the most of the opportunity of a lifetime.

While Rich and I were off gallivanting around in South America, my second cousin Neil Maskaant persuaded my parents to buy a box of a dietary supplement called Nutrilite. They began taking the vitamins on a regular basis and raved about them to us when we got back. At their urging, I allowed Neil to make an appointment with me to talk about Nutrilite products. At first, I wasn't enthusiastic. Pill peddling wasn't the sort of business to make much money in, I thought. Rich and I were poking around for another good business to add to Ja-Ri's menagerie, however, so I agreed to listen to what Neil had to offer. One night in August 1949, while Rich was out on a date, Neil and a partner of his came over from Chicago to give me the pitch. It turned out "peddling pills" was making cousin Neil a thousand dollars a month, which in 1949 was quite a good income. There was no significant investment involved, and no risk. Nutrilite sounded like it could be the sort of business Rich and I were looking for, so I wrote Neil a check for two boxes of Nutrilite and a sales kit. I made Neil understand that Rich and I were in business together and that if Rich didn't like the Nutrilite idea, he had to tear my check up. When Rich got back from his date that night, I showed him the boxes of Nutrilite and explained the Nutrilite program to him. He was skeptical too, but when I finished telling him what Neil had said, Rich was sold on the idea. The qualms some people have at the thought of selling vitamins disappear quickly when the prospect of making a lot of money enters the picture. Rich agreed to add the Nutrilite business to the other undertakings we had going at the time, and so we became Nutrilite distributors. We could never have guessed how far this simple decision would take us.

The next day we sold a box of Nutrilite to a man who ran a grocery store in Ada. That was a pretty easy sale because the old fellow liked us and was willing to help us get started. We found out soon, however, that success in this business was not going to be handed to us on a silver platter. When we talked to some of our friends about our new business, they thought we were crazy. Many people in those days thought vitamins were a waste of money. For two weeks, we couldn't sell a single box, and our Nutrilite distributorship went absolutely nowhere. With sales dead in the water, we began to think that perhaps we had made a mistake. A thousand dollars a month seemed like an impossibility, at the rate we were going. We began to forget about Neil and his boxes of pills, and our attention wandered to the other business interests we were pursuing.

Then Neil invited us to a meeting of Nutrilite distributors in Chicago. Rich and I drove down, thinking that if this meeting didn't give us some reason to stick with Nutrilite products, we'd probably quit. It was a larger meeting than I had suspected. One hundred and fifty respectable-looking people were there, all excited about selling vitamins, and many of them enjoying considerable success in their Nutrilite businesses. We talked to some men who had quit good jobs to sell Nutrilite products full-time and make more money. Others were just beginning, like us, but they had a zeal to sell Nutrilite that put us to shame. Speakers at the conference told about their success in Nutrilite and shared strategies for greater sales. To Rich and me, the whole Nutrilite idea started looking better and better.

GETTING SERIOUS

On the way home from Chicago, we decided to drop everything else we were doing and get serious with Nutrilite. We were so excited by the time we reached Grand Rapids that we pulled over into a gas station on Hall Street and subjected the fellow behind the counter to a high-energy sales talk. He bought a box, probably more as a friendly gesture than out of a desire for better nutrition.

Our first objective was to get a hundred customers. An average sale was $20, and if we could sell 100 to 120 boxes a month, our 40 or 50 percent of the total would come out to a thousand a month, just like Neil was making. There was always the possibility that we might get someone to sign up as a distributor, but product sales came first with Nutrilite. We put advertisements in weekly newspapers all around and personally called on people who responded. No secret success story here; just plain old direct selling.

Pretty soon we held our own sales meeting, in the basement of a restaurant at the Grand Rapids airport, to organize people who might be interested in becoming Nutrilite distributors. We weren't sure what to expect, but we thought that with all the advertising we had done we might get a hundred or more people. Instead, only eight people showed up. There was something odd about these eight people, too. They all arrived together, and none of them looked too happy to be there. I made a little welcoming speech and then we showed a little film about nutrition, which didn't seem to interest any of them. After we wrapped up our presentation, we were dismayed to see that there were no questions. No one seemed interested in the business. Instead, without a word, all eight stood and began filing out the door. Rich and I were flabbergasted. After all the thought and preparation we had put into this first meeting, this was a big letdown. Trying to imagine what we might have done wrong, we started packing up our things and putting the tables and chairs back in order. Then the door opened and we saw one of the eight enter. "You should probably know who we are," he said. "We're from the Nutrilite sales organization in this area. We saw your ad in the paper and thought we'd just come out and see what you fellows were up to." And without one word more, he did an about-face and stalked out.

That was doubly discouraging. Not only had our advertising been ineffective; now we knew there was established competition in the area. We persisted, however, continuing to advertise and hold meetings at the airport. We would show a film, then give a sales presentation, just as we did that first night. Rich then, as now, did most of the talking. I helped answer questions and tried to keep the cranky projector functioning. That disastrous first meeting was followed by other, more successful meetings, and the business began to grow. We built a small sales organization, which in the first year had a group retail sales volume of $85,000.

It wasn't easy. We used a selling strategy, however, that seemed to open doors for us. Rich and I would hand out a booklet called "How to Get Well and Stay Well." This was essentially a book of testimonials from people who said that Nutrilite had helped them conquer various illnesses, feel more energetic, and live a more fulfilling life. When we went back to pick up the booklet, we would make a presentation and possibly a sale.

About a year after we started with Nutrilite, Rich and I and some other distributors decided we'd like to see the Nutrilite facilities in California, so we all piled in a couple of cars and drove west. We mainly wanted to see if this outfit we had joined had anything substantial behind it, so we stopped at one of the Nutrilite farms and toured the factory. I thought it all quite impressive at the time, though it was a relatively small plant by most standards. But we began to realize with that visit the importance of maintaining distributor confidence through visits to headquarters.

As Rich and I gained experience, we put on bigger and better sales meetings. Many of them were very successful. Some of those who entered our sales organization through those early gatherings quickly built large distributorships, and our business gained momentum. Not all of the meetings worked out as we planned, however. Once Rich and I put on a big sales meeting in Lansing, Michigan. We advertised on the radio, put big ads in the newspaper, and passed out brochures on the street. The auditorium had two hundred seats, and with all the publicity work we had done we began to wonder if that would be enough. This could be the beginning of something big, we thought.

That night, two people showed up. It was terribly awkward giving a sales presentation to just two people in a room with two hundred seats. We probably sounded a little less than enthusiastic. Late that night, we drove back to Grand Rapids. Disheartened, I asked Rich if he thought we should continue with Nutrilite. "If we can't do any better than that with all the publicity we did, maybe we should just drop the whole thing." For a moment Rich hung his head. Then I saw a look of fierce determination come over his face. "Nonsense!" he said. "We can't quit just because we had one down night! We know this can work! Besides, we already have some distributors who look like they could blow the lid off the sales volume we're doing now." Chided, I turned my thoughts to planning our next meeting. This was the optimistic, tenacious Rich I knew, and it wasn't the first time he had encouraged me to persist when things began to look a little bad. In fact, if you're looking for "insider information" on how we became successful, you could start with two words: persistence and enthusiasm.

Although Rich and I were new to the direct-selling industry, we soon found that we could be successful if we followed a few simple rules. First, we had to believe in our product. No one is going to believe that they need what you're selling if you don't genuinely convey a personal belief that the product works for you. Nutrilite is effective—we were convinced of that. To this day I take Nutrilite products as a dietary supplement, and I truly believe it has given me a greater measure of health through the years. We would never have purchased the Nutrilite Company in 1972 if we didn't have that faith in the product. Today, Amway distributors are all encouraged to use Amway products in their homes, because people who personally use and trust those products are better able to communicate their benefits to customers. In fact, if you know someone who sells Amway products but doesn't use them, let me know!

Our second rule was to have determination to succeed. Every business has its downturns. Many would-be entrepreneurs give up at the first sign of trouble. Quitting the first time a problem presents itself is not a way to prevent failure; it is a way to assure it. Patience will be rewarded. Most of the time, if the basic business idea is sound, a downturn will prove to be only temporary, and short-term losses will turn into long-term gains.

A third rule of success, we learned, was personal involvement in the business. We had to know what was going on in our sales organization in order to make good decisions about products and policies. We had to be in touch with individual employees and Nutrilite distributors in order to keep ourselves informed. Rich and I began the tradition of keeping in contact with employees through monthly "Speak Up" meetings. Rotating groups of employees from different parts of the company were encouraged to come and "speak up" if there was some problem they'd like for us to address. Not only could we become aware of problems in the company, we could glean some great ideas from these meetings. Today, my son Steve and Rich's son Dick continue this tradition as chairman and president. Rich and I have for decades maintained contact with our top distributors through meetings on board the *Enterprise,* Amway's famous luxury yacht. Not only do the cruises provide a reward for high attainment in Amway, they give us feedback on policies and fresh ideas for new products. Keeping in touch with distributors on a daily basis is easier now than ever before with new technology—a voice-mail system called Amvox allows the Amway corporate leadership to communicate with each distributor, providing news, encouragement, and advice. We stuck with Nutrilite because we saw that it had potential. Rich and I had dropped other business ventures, like the toy company, when they didn't work out, and we were willing to drop Nutrilite if we saw that it would not succeed. But we saw something unique in Nutrilite that persuaded us that it would work, if we were willing to put the necessary work into it.

FOCUS: THE INDIVIDUAL

Nutrilite had a decentralized organizational structure that appealed to us. In ordinary firms, the rewards to the individual are typically limited by the success of the company as a whole. Further, individual creativity tends to be suppressed in a centralized organizational structure. Centralization has some benefits, to be sure. It helps to have one group of people doing all the production, while another group does the accounting, another group does the product design and research, and another group handles legal affairs. But centralization has definite drawbacks. Microcontrol of the individual worker by dozens of managers and committees and vice presidents can't help but crush creativity in the very areas where it is most needed. The thousands of brilliant people who leave megafirms each year to start their own businesses know about the stifling effects of a rigid corporate structure. In Nutrilite, each distributor had his own business, but he was supported by a company that handled only those functions best performed by a more centralized organization. In this way Nutrilite managed to bring out the best in human creativity through direct selling while taking advantage of large-scale economies in research, production, and other areas. These benefits filtered down to the customer in the form of higher-quality products and personal service.

Nutrilite's organizational form was often compared to a pyramid. In this it was really no different from more traditional firms. In an ordinary firm, there is a small, well-paid group at the top composed of the chairman, president, vice presidents, and so on. Under these people is a larger group of managers, and under the managers is the largest group of all—the technicians, clerks, computer operators, secretaries, and laborers. Draw that out on a sheet of paper and a rather neat-looking pyramid emerges. The military is structured in the same way. There's nothing sinister about the shape. Nutrilite actually had a more fluid form in its marketing division than traditional corporations. What distinguished Nutrilite was the focus on individuals, not groups of employees. Individuals retained control over the way they ran their distributorship, because it was their distributorship, and no one else's. Unlike a traditional business in which each level has the ability to give orders to the level below, Nutrilite's distributor structure maintained the independence of each person while rewarding cooperation and emulation. Also, individual incentives were enhanced so that rewards matched performance. Upward mobility didn't depend on how well one was able to impress a manager or vice president; it depended only on personal achievement. And anyone could start a Nutrilite distributorship. No résumés, interviews, college degrees, background checks, or previous selling experience required. With a moderately priced box of vitamins and some introductory literature, anyone could be in business for himself.

Anyone who has started a traditional business can tell of the large amount of funds necessary to begin operations. Usually, this means appealing to banks, friends, and relatives for investment capital. Sometimes this works out for the entrepreneur, but saddling a new business with a large amount of debt puts it at a disadvantage and can lead to its early fail-ure. Nutrilite's system provided a way around those potential problems by keeping start-up costs very low. If the Nutrilite distributorship somehow didn't work out, there were no credi-tors to pay off, no expensive assets to liquidate, no threat of bankruptcy. The capital-intensive manufacturing side of the business was handled by a separate organization to keep those costs off the backs of the individual distributors.

Rich and I were sure that Nutrilite was onto something that could be extremely successful. So whenever things began look-ing dismal, we reminded ourselves that the Nutrilite approach made sense and would come through for us if we worked hard and gave it some time. When we started Amway years later, we patterned its basic organizational marketing plan after Nutrilite's, making improvements where we thought they were necessary.

The decentralization principle that made Nutrilite work, and that makes Amway work today, carries over into the polit-ical sphere. There are certain things that centralized govern-ment can do well, such as provide national defense, justice, and protection from crime. Many activities, however, are best done by decentralized human institutions like families and local churches. When centralized government tries to take over the functions of families, churches, businesses, and individuals, all of society suffers. Human ingenuity and creativity is squelched, and those things formerly done by decentralized institutions are done poorly or not done at all.

Soon, however, we would learn that even the best structure and environment isn't much help if integrity becomes an issue.

CHAPTER 5

Why Integrity Matters

Although our Nutrilite business was going fairly well, the national Nutrilite organization was having major problems. Nutrilite was actually two companies: Nutrilite Products, Inc., which manufactured the products, and Mytinger and Casselberry, which ran the distributor organization of which we were a part. For many years these two companies had worked harmoniously together, but in the late 1950s the relationship began to deteriorate.

At the heart of the problem was a case the Food and Drug Administration brought against Nutrilite in the early 1950s for alleged unfair or excessive claims of product efficacy. To fend off the FDA, Nutrilite hired an attorney named Charles Ryan.

When the FDA demanded all of Nutrilite's records that pertained to the case, Charlie turned the tables on the FDA and demanded all of their records. The FDA protested, claiming that, by virtue of being a government agency, they didn't have to supply their records. Eventually, that dispute ended up at the Supreme Court, where it was decided in Nutrilite's favor. As soon as that decision came down, the FDA decided they wanted to settle with Nutrilite. In the 1950s, no one quite knew what path the vitamin industry would take or how big it would become. Certainly the medical profession was concerned that vitamins, which were of course nonprescription, would become a competitor to traditional medicine. The big pharmaceutical firms were none too pleased, either. To the FDA and the traditional medical-care industry, Nutrilite was a little fly in the ointment.

The result of the case was a 1955 FDA ruling that forced a change in Nutrilite's advertising policies. Thanks to Charlie, Nutrilite was still able to operate, but the company was essentially prohibited from making claims about the product and from using testimonials. Of course, this reduced selling effectiveness. Testimonials, like those in the book "How to Get Well and Stay Well" had been the most effective way of selling the product, and revenues started drying up. It's difficult to sell anything if you can't tell people that it works.

Someone at Nutrilite came up with the idea of diversifying into cosmetics, so that if the FDA managed to permanently damage the vitamin side of the business, there would be another revenue source to keep things going. So Nutrilite launched the Edith Rehnborg line of cosmetics and started selling them directly to the distributors instead of going through Mytinger and Casselberry.

Then the whole matter of the contract between Mytinger and Casselberry and Nutrilite Products, Inc., blew up. Mytinger and Casselberry was bound to buy all its products from Nutrilite, for selling through the sales organization. This led to a dispute over who actually owned the sales organization—Mytinger and Casselberry or Nutrilite Products. Nutrilite tried to attract distributors to its side, creating a near fatal rift in the distributor organization. As soon as the fight started, people stopped selling the products (which were more difficult to sell anyway because of the FDA ruling) and waited to see what the outcome would be. The owner of Nutrilite, Carl Rehnborg, was losing control of his company. The managers he had hired had their own goals for Nutrilite, and they began fighting one another for dominance. Making matters worse was the necessary downsizing of the company, which created even more internal tension and distracted the leadership even further from selling the product. Carl, deeply attached to his limited product line and suffering under crushing regulatory pressure, was not as effective as he might have been in solving these problems. He was a visionary, he had a strong entrepreneurial drive, and he had a good product idea, but he was hindered by poor managers. In 1958, Mytinger and Casselberry formed a nine-man study group of distributors to come up with solutions to these problems, and I was made the chairman. We enjoyed some success in resolving the differences between Nutrilite and the sales organization, but I did not hold great hopes for the future of Nutrilite. Nutrilite was pushing to go into cosmetics, and Mytinger and Casselberry were very reluctant to do so. Also, Mytinger and Casselberry and the Nutrilite leadership were setting a very poor precedent for future cooperation. Lee Mytinger and Bill Casselberry weren't getting along well, and the second generation of leaders—Mytinger's son and Casselberry's son-in-law—weren't doing well either under the circumstances. None of the Mytingers or Casselberrys were getting along with Carl Rehnborg. The whole situation deteriorated into finger-pointing. Rich and I were sure that, even though the study group had resolved some of the current problems, some difficulty would surely arise in the future that the leadership would be unable to cope with. At the root of the problems was a lack of trust between Nutrilite, Mytinger and Casselberry, and some of the distributors, and this was nearly impossible to repair. Our problems with Nutrilite weren't with Carl Rehnborg himself. He was a great man, and I had quite a lot of contact with Carl even after Rich and I started Amway. Carl could discourse intelligently on a variety of topics, astronomy being one of his favorites. He was a fascinating man to be around, and my dinner conversations with him were always edifying. Because Rich and I always respected his work in the nutrition field, Amway recently endowed the Carl F. Rehnborg Professorship in Disease Prevention at Stanford University's School of Medicine. (Carl's son, Sam, received his doctorate at Stanford, hence the connection.)

Nutrilite's actions taught Rich and me the importance of mutual trust in doing business. The leadership had violated some pretty basic principles, and in so doing had alienated its distributors. With any multilevel-marketing business, it is important to maintain clear lines of sponsorship. That is, if Ed introduces Joe to the business opportunity, or sponsors Joe, then Joe can't go buy his products from another distributor. This rule keeps distributors from trying to steal sales organizations (and markets) from other distributors, and makes sure that those who go out and do the sponsoring receive the rewards for their efforts. Nutrilite began breaking lines of sponsorship right and left, the problem eventually becoming so serious that Rich and I began looking for some way to protect the distributors under us. Trust is a fragile thing, like fine china. Drop it, and it will break. Glue may patch it back together, but the cracks will always show. Break faith with someone, and he will be reluctant to trust you the next time.

At one point in the arbitration process between Nutrilite and its distributors, Carl offered me the position of president of Nutrilite. It was a tempting offer. The job would have paid a lot more than I was making as a Nutrilite distributor, but I turned it down. There before me was a secure, steady income and the opportunity to attempt some real changes in Nutrilite. The task was not beyond me—in helping to resolve the dispute between the Nutrilite leadership and Mytinger and Casselberry I think I had demonstrated some measure of capability in a leadership position. The loss of my independence was too much for me to accept, however. It was important to Rich and to me to be self-employed, to set our own courses and make decisions that would truly be our own. Even in a high-level position at Nutrilite, I would be an employee, limited in my ability to do what I thought was best and at the mercy of someone else's decisions. Rich and I also considered the impact that my new job might have on our friendship and partnership. If I were to become president of Nutrilite, we could preserve some aspects of our partnership. Rich could have come on board into the Nutrilite management as chief operating officer, or in some other capacity. But some things would undoubtedly have changed, and not all in a way we would prefer.

BUSINESS ETHICS BASICS

From the very beginning of our work with Nutrilite, Rich and I sought to run our sales organization according to biblical principles of integrity, faithfulness, and truthfulness. When we started Amway, we held to the same ethical standards. Knowing that we were dependent upon God for the ability to do what was right, we bathed our activities in private prayer. All of our corporate meetings were opened with prayer, and Rich and I were quietly breathing prayers all the time. We believe it was effective. Without God's grace, Amway would never have been successful.

A business without integrity will be penalized in the marketplace. If a business's products don't meet the claims of its advertisers, or if product quality is inconsistent, the business will lose customers to its competitors. Skilled employees, frustrated with internal policies, depart for other jobs. On the other hand, a firm known for its integrity will be rewarded by increased demand for its products and greater customer and employee loyalty.

A great side benefit of integrity is trust. If you can believe someone, you can trust him, and that's probably what helped establish a policy Rich and I have had regarding our business decisions. On the one hand, we never proceed with any new direction unless both of us agreed on it. On the other hand, because we trusted each other so much, we agreed that whenever one of us was gone, the other was in charge. Completely.

For example, one year I was about to leave for a month's vacation. We were planning a new cafeteria for employees, and before I left on my vacation I explained to contractor Dan Vos how the cafeteria was to be built. After I left for my vacation, Dan started work on the cafeteria, only to run into Rich, who wanted some fairly substantial changes in the plans. Dan protested, telling Rich that my orders had been different. "Dan, that doesn't mean a thing," said Rich. "Jay isn't here now, and our policy is that when one of us is gone, the other is boss. So you do it this way!" Dan was taken aback by the sudden change in plans, but Rich knew that I would go along with his changes, whatever they were. I trusted Rich to use his own good judgment, just as he trusts me, and Rich knew I would never criticize him for doing what he thought was right in my absence. Dan was never called back to change the cafeteria to its original specifications, and no one ever heard us arguing about it. Because our partnership had integrity, we trusted each other to always act in the best interest of the company.

At this point in our relationship with Nutrilite, however, our faith in the business was in question. Little did we know that it was about to get worse, forcing Rich and me to make an important decision that would change our lives together.

CHAPTER 6

Taking the Plunge

By 1958, Rich and I had built a strong, healthy sales organization with Nutrilite products, but our five thousand distributors were angry. The infighting among the Nutrilite leadership began to take its toll, and morale and sales both began to drop. The FDA's ruling was having a serious effect as well, and the tension increased. Some of our distributors were even talking about leaving Nutrilite altogether. All of us had made a considerable investment of our time and energy in Nutrilite, and between the Nutrilite leadership and the federal government, that investment was being threatened with total destruction. Something had to be done, and done quickly.

The Ja-Ri sales organization could be saved, we thought, if

we could reduce our reliance on Nutrilite products. Dropping Nutrilite vitamin sales altogether was out of the question. If we could get our distributors to expand their offerings, however, the failure of the Nutrilite leadership would not destroy the sales organization. This would not be an easy task. Many Nutrilite distributors were so loyal to the one product that we wondered whether they would sell anything else. We had to structure our diversification very carefully, making sure the timing and the new products were just right. Rich and I were fully aware of the risks—it could be that none of the distributors of Nutrilite food supplement would want to change anything at all. We had to catch them turning the corner, so disgusted with Nutrilite leadership that they were ready to transfer their allegiance, but not so disgusted that they weren't going to do any selling at all.

In the summer of 1958 we held a meeting of our top distributors in Charlevoix, Michigan. There we announced our plans to cut our reliance on Nutrilite by developing a new product line. "You've put in a lot of long hours building a business around the Nutrilite Food Supplement," we told them, "but the management there has made some moves that have shaken your faith in them. We think you can use your organization to sell other products in addition to Nutrilite. We'll provide you with management who'll improve the business opportunity developed in Nutrilite and enable you to get a substantial return out of the investment in time and energy that you put into your Nutrilite business."

We couldn't force anyone in our sales organization to go along with us. Nutrilite distributors were independent, just as Amway distributors are today. So we gave each person in our group the opportunity to stay with us or to continue dealing entirely with Nutrilite. This was a real test for Rich and me, because their decision depended on whether they trusted our judgment and leadership. If they decided not to go along with us, it was back to square one for us. Fortunately, every person at that Charlevoix meeting decided to strike out in a new direction with us. These loyal individuals would form the nucleus of our new direct-selling venture.

Word spread quickly, and it wasn't long before Nutrilite distributors in other sales organizations wanted to join us. At first, we refused to admit them because we didn't want to raid Nutrilite and take their sales force at a time when they were weak. Finally, after several years, we allowed people from other Nutrilite sales groups to join us, but we kept their lines of sponsorship intact.

WHAT TO SELL

Rich and I put a lot of thought into what product line to add. Whatever it was, it had to be something anyone could sell. A Nutrilite sale required a one-hour presentation to convince the potential customer of their need for dietary supplements. Our new product line had to be something everyone knew they needed. Remembering Nutrilite's devastating confrontation with the federal government, we decided that we also needed something that was not highly regulated. Today we would be hard pressed to find a single product that meets that criterion, but in the late 1950s, there were still some products relatively untouched by federal or state regulation.

We picked cleaning products, and in the four decades hence they have proven a good choice. For better or worse, Amway is today identified with soap more than any other product we sell. In picking something that was easy to sell, we made something of a breakthrough in direct selling. To this day, Amway has followed the principle of marketing products that have a broad appeal and are sold with a minimum of effort.

Our first product was a concentrated biodegradable cleaner called Frisk, which later became our Liquid Organic

Concentrate, or LOC All-Purpose Cleaner. We had seen the problems that could occur when depending on a third-party manufacturer, so one of the first goals we set was to manufacture our products ourselves. Though that was impractical at first for a beginning company, we became even more convinced of its importance when one of our first suppliers fell out on us. As a replacement, early in 1960 we began purchasing our liquid cleaner from Atco Manufacturing Co. of Detroit. To make sure we could depend on this new supplier, we bought a 50 percent interest in the company. As half owners of the firm, we were able to persuade Atco to change its name to "Amway Manufacturing Corporation" and move to Ada later that year. Now, if you visit Amway World Headquarters in Ada, Michigan, you can see our enormous factory-office complex along the "Mile of Amway" on M-21, where many Amway products are manufactured today.

The keystone of our new venture was the Sales and Marketing Plan, which has become known fondly in Amway circles as, simply, the "Plan." The Plan was based roughly on the Nutrilite structure, but we made several significant modifications to avoid the problems that Nutrilite had developed and improve individual incentives. Rich and I laid out a big sheet of butcher paper on my kitchen floor and started figuring out how we could send financial rewards directly to the hardest workers. Each business owner, in the Sales and Marketing Plan, has an incentive to sell products and to build a sales organization of his own that will sell even more products. The more an individual sells, the more he makes, and the more that individual's sales organization sells, the more he makes. No one makes a dime unless products are sold.

When we brought our Nutrilite sales organization into Amway, we preserved all the lines of sponsorship so that none of our distributors lost their position in the transition. We even put Neil Maaskant, my cousin, who had introduced us to

Nutrilite, over Ja-Ri in the new organization. It was only fair to do so—Neil had brought us into the business and, as we saw it, was entitled to part of the proceeds as long as we were selling Nutrilite. Neil and his wife passed on a number of years ago, but their estate continues to receive income from their interest in the business.

In our efforts to automatically move money to the worker, the plan we devised became unavoidably complex. As Amway boomed, it became impossible for Amway clerks with adding machines to keep track of all the individual and group sales. Today, giant computers at Amway headquarters run twenty-four hours a day calculating individual product sales and group sales volume and printing out bonus checks for over two million Amway distributors worldwide. The Plan is essentially unchanged after all these years, though we have had to add several levels at the top for those distributors who achieved sales in excess of our predictions.

Fundamental to the Amway Sales and Marketing Plan from the very beginning was the importance of the line of sponsorship. The sour experience we had with Nutrilite had made a powerful impression on Rich and me, and we made sure that the lines of sponsorship were well protected. We have devoted a lot of effort over the years to keeping it that way. Amway distributors have appreciated that, I think. They know that their hard work will pay off, because Amway won't break faith with them. Years after starting Amway, we purchased a controlling amount of stock in Nutrilite for $22 million. This allowed us to sell their high-quality dietary supplements without losing that measure of control we deemed so essential in 1959, and it provided Nutrilite distributors with the option of selling the whole line of Amway products.

Amway's beginnings were modest. In April of 1959 the "American Way Association" began as a new division of Ja-Ri in the basements of our two homes on Windy Hill in Ada. My basement was the office, and Rich's was the warehouse. To save money, we shared a common telephone line and used a buzzer to signal each other when to pick up. I spent many hours that year in my basement, as I wrote sales manuals, ran them off on the mimeograph machine, and collated them on the Ping-Pong table.

Our wives were not as convinced as we were about our chances for success, but they were actively helpful from the start. Also with us from the beginning were Walter and Evelyn Bass, Fred and Bernice Hansen, Joe and Heleyn Victor, George and Eleanor Tietsma, and Jere Dutt, among others. Our first employee was Kay Evans, a part-time secretary. As the business grew that first year, we quickly realized that we would need a new corporate structure and a catchier, easier-to-remember name. So in November of 1959, we formed the Amway Sales Corporation to procure and inventory products, to sell them to distributors, and to administer the Sales and Marketing Plan. To handle group insurance and other benefits for the distributor organization, we also formed the Amway Services Corporation.

Any businessman will tell you that the first three years of starting a business are the most trying. In our case, we were starting with the benefit of an intact sales organization for selling Nutrilite. Rich and I had had experience setting up businesses, which proved invaluable when setting up Amway. We recalled to mind all of our past successes and failures—the Wolverine Air Service days, the drive-in restaurant, Stone Mill Products, Grand Rapids Toy Company, and most recently, Nutrilite. We didn't know if this new venture would be a success like the air service or a dud like the toy company. The direct-selling industry was an immature industry in the 1950s, and there was not a set way of going about this kind of business. We were pioneers, in a sense, and learning had to be by trial and error. Early on, we made a lot of changes, trying this and that to see what worked best.

Eventually, the question of titles came up, and we handled that one with in our usual pragmatic manner: We took turns. One year, Rich would be chairman and I would be president, and the next year I would be chairman and Rich would be president. This worked for a few years, until our lawyers told us that we needed to decide once and for all—this was needlessly complicating matters. So Rich and I talked about it for a couple of minutes, and finally Rich said, "Jay, you're the oldest, so you be the chairman."

HANDS-ON EXPERIENCE

We experimented with several products early on. LOC, or Liquid Organic Concentrate, was our mainstay for a while, but we diversified as soon as we could. Our laundry detergent, SA-8, was an early and lasting addition to our product line. Soon after, we added cookware and home water-softening equipment. Other ventures were not so successful. We even sold bomb shelters and electric generators, which only makes sense if you were around during the tense cold war years. We never sold many of these, probably because our Sales and Marketing Plan was not well suited at that time to products that required installation and maintenance expertise.

Rich and I also took hands-on approach with new product development. Once when we were trying out different formulas for an automobile polish, we used one of my cars as a laboratory. Rich and I took several bottles out to my driveway and rubbed the different concoctions on various spots on my car. The one that shined the brightest and repelled dirt the longest became our famous Silicone Glaze. My car never did look the same after the experiments we performed on it, though!

By the way, getting your hands dirty seems to be a key ingredient to the entrepreneurial life. George Gilder's book, *The Spirit of Enterprise,* tells the story of Thomas J. Fatjo, who entered the garbage collection business in a hands-on way in the mid-1960s. Believing that the solid-waste disposal business was about to take off, he bought a garbage truck and began driving it door to door in Houston, Texas. One morning the compactor broke down with seventy more houses to go. Not one to leave his customers unserved, Fatjo jumped into the bin and began stomping down the garbage with his own two feet. Armpit deep in refuse, Fatjo probably wondered whether this business was worth continuing. He persisted, however, to create Browning-Ferris Industries, the world's largest solid-waste disposal firm. Fourteen years after his unenviable battle with the trash compactor, Fatjo's company had half a billion dollars in revenues and was listed on the New York Stock Exchange. Today Fatjo credits his hands-on experience in the waste collection business with Browning-Ferris's astounding growth.

We met a few people early on who stayed on with us and have participated in our growth for decades. One of those was Wally Buttrick, who as a seventeen-year-old student at Lowell High School was earning spending money by mowing lawns in Ada. Impressed by the vigorous effort he put into grass cutting, I offered him a job as a mimeograph machine operator. He tackled that job with all the energy he had, and we soon had him doing all kinds of office work as the business expanded.

Wally soon graduated from high school and took a college preparatory class, but things were going so well at Amway that he decided not to enter college then. As Amway grew and prospered, we put Wally in charge of the large new print shop, which he headed until 1963. At that point we made him a field coordination manager and gave him some additional responsibility. By the next year, at the age of twenty-one, Wally had fifteen people working under him. Soon after that, we promoted him again to head an important department.

From inside Amway, Wally watched distributors reach high levels of achievement and become wealthy. After about nine years of working as an Amway employee, he decided that he wanted a piece of the action, and Wally became a distributor. Wally, being the hardworking fellow that he is, soon made that into a very successful business and quit his job at Amway. As pleased as we were with his success as a distributor, we were sorry to lose such a wonderful employee. Wally's departure provoked what became known as the "Wally Buttrick Rule," which kept salaried Amway employees from becoming distributors. That rule has now been relaxed, but it was a unique part of Amway history.

Apart from all the individuals who helped make Amway what it is today, several companies were indispensable in those first years. Amway never would have survived had it not been for the help of Michigan National Bank and the forbearance of Monsanto Chemical. To all appearances, we were not a good credit risk in 1959, or for several years after that. Michigan National lent to us when no other bank would. Monsanto Chemical, a large supplier early on, retained us as a customer when other suppliers would have lost their patience. I recall a visit by Monsanto's regional sales manager one day just one or two years after Amway began. We told him of our small progress, of our hopes for the future, and of our lack of ready cash. But he must have thought we could make it, for he agreed to sell us all we needed, giving us a generous sixty days from delivery to pay.

We were not in good financial shape for several years, so we were reluctant to provide Monsanto complete details of our condition. Once, after we had stalled for a whole year on giving Monsanto a profit statement, their credit manager came down to look us over. After a bit of arm-twisting on his part, we showed him our profit statement. It showed a net worth of $10,000. At the time, we owed Monsanto about $60,000. Several years later, when Amway was in much better shape, that same man came over to Ada to give us an award for buying over one million pounds of raw material from Monsanto in a month's time. He asked us then if we recalled the day we gave him that first profit statement. "When I saw what your net worth was," he said, "and thought of what you owed us, I never thought I'd see this day!" For Monsanto, patience with a struggling new customer paid off when we gained our footing. For Amway, that forbearance meant the difference between survival and shutting down operations. To this day Amway does business with Monsanto and Michigan National Bank, because loyalty to old friends is something I still believe in.

Earlier, I introduced you to another early business partner, contractor Dan Vos. In 1960 we were thinking about moving Amway into an abandoned forty-by-sixty-foot gas station in Ada, and Rich was standing outside looking it over (and probably trying to figure out where the first addition would go!). When Dan drove by in one of his company pickups, Rich saw the Vos Construction lettering on the side and flagged him down. The two men got to talking, and Rich asked Dan to put in a door to a bathroom and build some additional shelving in the old building. It was a minor job, one that most contractors wouldn't have bothered with, but Dan sent two men out with a truck to do the work that afternoon. Little did Dan know that that small job would lead to tens of millions of dollars of construction work over the next four decades. That first job was followed by other jobs, each successively larger, and each one done on a handshake and a promise. First there was a forty-by-sixty-foot addition to the back of the building, doubling the size of Amway's new home. A very short while later, Dan built another addition that doubled the size again. Only a few weeks after Dan Vos built those shelves in the old gas station, he built a 5,600-square-foot manufacturing facility for us. The next year we gave him six new building projects. By the end of 1964, Dan had built four new warehouses, a twenty-thousand-square-foot office building, a tank farm, a cluster of storage silos, and eight or ten additions to existing buildings.

As Amway continued to grow, we continued to enlist Dan Vos's talents. There never could have been a more efficient building program—it was all built on trust in one another. Today the Amway physical plant and office facilities total 4.2 million square feet, divided among eighty separate buildings. Almost all of that has been built by Vos Construction, almost all without formal contracts or lawyers. The faithfulness runs both ways. We have never had any major problems with Dan Vos's work. Dan shares with Rich and me the belief that businessmen should do their work well, doing it all to the glory of God. There are many ways that a businessman can glorify God through his work—for Dan Vos, part of that was following through on promises and doing quality work. Dan also had a commitment to local churches. Before he retired, Dan's company had built over a hundred church buildings.

Amway was soon far beyond its humble origins, and Rich and I adapted to the new needs of the company. Amway's startling growth rate tried our leadership capabilities, but we kept things running smoothly with the help of a man named Clair Knox. Clair's number one job was to make sure that Rich and I didn't get off on the wrong track with the business. He would spot potential trouble coming down the road and head it off by calling Rich and me into a little conference. If Rich and I began ignoring an important issue, Clair would end that by forcing us to resolve those issues before they became real problems. His work was probably more beneficial than either of us realized at the time.

As Amway expanded, Rich and I developed our own unique areas of expertise. Rich naturally took to motivational speaking and distributor relations, while I began developing a facility with financial analysis and internal affairs. It's not as though we sat down and said, "OK, I'll take care of international expansion and you take care of research and development," and so on. It was more of an understanding that we had—we each understood where the strengths of the other lay, so we each made room for the other to use those strengths to his fullest potential. The specialization we worked out helped Amway run smoothly for decades.

AVERTING DESTRUCTION

Just before midnight on a warm Friday night in July 1969, I was sitting in my living room reading when I was startled by a thunderous boom outside that rattled my windows. At first I thought the noise was a sonic boom from a military aircraft, but that would have been unusual over Ada, Michigan. As I rose and stepped toward the front window I noticed an ominous orange glow above the trees toward the north. My heart pounded once, very hard, and my throat contracted in fear as I realized that the glow was likely from the Amway factory complex less than half a mile away. My telephone rang, and I snatched it up to hear Bernard Schaafsma giving me dreadful news. There had been an explosion in the east wing of the Amway factory, in the aerosol division. My head spun. Rich was on his boat up at Charlevoix, Michigan. "Call Rich," I told him. "I'm on my way." Dressing quickly, I told Betty what had happened, got in my car, and drove through Ada toward Amway. As I came into view of the Amway factory, I was horrified to see that flames were leaping sixty feet into the air over what had been one of the most fire-prone parts of the building. I thought of the tank farm of petroleum derivatives several hundred feet from the east wall of the aerosol division and stepped on the gas. A sheriff's deputy stopped me at the east gate. He found out it was my factory that was burning down and waved me through.

The fire trucks had arrived only four or five minutes before me and were still hooking up their hoses. It appeared that the roof of the almost-new aerosol division had collapsed, and underneath it was a hellish red-orange inferno. The roar of burning gas was deafening. Two truck trailers and a tanker truck had been driven away from the building at great risk by employees Clayton Jastifer, George Simington, and George McManis, preventing further damage and the possibility of another explosion. Several other employees were about to enter an adjoining office building to rescue some important files, but I stopped them. "Forget the papers," I said. "Get the people out!"

Dan Vos arrived a few minutes later. When he heard over the radio that the Amway complex was on fire, he sped over, only to be met by a policeman at the Ada Bridge who told him he'd have to turn around because of the fire. "I am going to get there," he said. "I built that place and you can't stop me!" When Dan saw his handiwork engulfed in flames, he burst into tears. "I know you shouldn't have that much love for a building," he told me later, "but to see your work burn to the ground tears at your heart." By God's mercy no one was killed in the blaze, although seventeen were injured, two seriously. The fire did more than half a million dollars in damage and totally destroyed 14,400 square feet of our 450,000-square-foot facility. The sprinkler system was rendered useless by the initial blast, but, for the most part, other fire safety measures worked to keep the fire confined.

When I saw that the fire was under control and that the injured were being cared for, I turned to Dan and said, "I'm going home. It's under control and there's nothing more for me to do here." He probably wondered how I could go home with my business burning up, but I didn't go home to sleep—I went home to work. New suppliers had to be found, a new aerosol division had to be constructed, and jobs for the aerosol plant employees had to be found for the meantime. The next morning at seven o'clock management was called together, and we set to work.

Today Amway has its own "fire department," and some employees take special courses in fire prevention and suppression to keep the 1969 disaster from repeating itself. Our firemen are well known for their professionalism and are occasionally called upon to assist the Ada municipal fire brigade.

Unfortunately, some "fires" take more than a top-gun fire brigade to knock down, as we were about to learn.

CHAPTER 7

Attack on Amway

One night, around midnight, the phone rang at my home in Ada. It was a distant cousin of mine. I didn't know her personally, but I had seen her occasionally at family gatherings and knew who she was. About twenty years old, she had been married only a few months. She was crying. She didn't know who else to turn to so she called me.

She and her husband had pooled all their savings and they had bought an interest in a pyramid plan for $4,000. The attorney general of Michigan had moved in on the scheme, and the plan operator had called a meeting in Lansing of all the plan holders to come around for a second helping.

Somehow the plan's promoters managed to stand up there

and tell these people that to save their original money they would have to make another contribution. There was nothing I could tell my cousin except not to throw good money after bad and to hope that the authorities might force a return of some of her money.

They were selling people a distributorship to sell distributorships to other people. A distributorship with any company, however, can only achieve value through the sale of useful products. A distributorship by itself is not instant money; you have to work.

This latest scheme that trapped my cousin, carried the sale of distributorships to the ultimate end. They eliminated the products. Instead of selling products, the distributor was supposed to sell an idea, a program that would convince anybody he could be great and make a lot of money.

In the 1960s and the 1970s there was a rash of operations like this that came to be known as pyramid schemes. These organizations attracted the naive and unsuspecting by promising fabulous returns on an initial investment with little effort—all the members had to do was recruit two or three others who would make the same investment. A few people at the very top could become very wealthy through scams like these by bilking those in the chain under them. Pyramid schemes would race through a community, until the last ones to join would find themselves with no one to recruit.

These sorts of scams have done Amway a lot of damage because Amway is often confused with pyramid schemes. We suffered from guilt by association. It is true that the organizational structure of Amway and other network marketing firms can be described as a pyramid, but so can any traditional business structure, or the military, or charitable organizations. What is important is that the Amway Sales and Marketing Plan lacks all of the distinguishing features of an illegal pyramid scheme.

The public, of course, doesn't always make the distinction. There was so much bad publicity surrounding the various scams that some people were saying that all direct selling should be made illegal. Killing the direct-selling industry would certainly get rid of pyramid schemes, but it would also destroy the 2,500 or so reputable direct-selling businesses in the country. So we launched a publicity campaign to educate the American public on the nature of illegal pyramid schemes and how to avoid them. Amway took out hundreds of ads in newspapers across the country, and I tried to communicate the problem in dozens of speeches I made to business and community organizations nationwide.

CHALLENGED BY GOVERNMENT

Educating the American public is one thing. Educating federal bureaucrats is quite a different task. We were forced to take on the challenge, however, when in 1975 the Federal Trade Commission filed an official complaint against Amway. The FTC charged that Amway's Sales and Marketing Plan was "a scheme to pyramid distributors upon ever-increasing numbers of other distributors," that it was "doomed to failure," and that it contained an "intolerable potential to deceive." We were charged with price-fixing (meaning that we were telling distributors at what prices they could sell their products), with restricting the activities of distributors by preventing them from selling Amway products through retail stores, and with misrepresenting the potential opportunities for success. The FTC's charges were the first serious assault on Amway—they threatened the very existence of our corporation. We eventually came out winners, but the attack convinced us of the importance of keeping the federal government apprised of who we were and what we were doing over here in Ada, Michigan.

Price-fixing charges were not entirely unusual. Before antitrust laws began outlawing such things, some firms would require independent distributors or retailers to charge certain prices for their products. This practice, called resale price maintenance, ensured, among other things, that a higher level of customer service would accompany the sale of the product.

At some point, every company had to change their policies on pricing—that's why you see the "suggested retail price" on boxes of merchandise today. Again, the unique nature of the Amway organization resulted in problems with regulators unfamiliar with the way Amway worked. The "restraint of trade" that was alleged to result from the modest set of rules we imposed on distributors was not an unusual charge either.

The whole situation could have been resolved in a thirty-minute meeting if we had been dealing with reasonable people, but regulatory agencies are not known for their reasonableness or efficiency. So the FTC sifted through manuals and over a hundred price lists that we had published at one time or another and tried to find one or two that they could construe as "price-fixing." Much of the FTC's evidence included publications and practices discontinued long before the trial. The FTC partly relied upon a 1963 Amway manual that required resale price maintenance. We argued, however, that Amway hadn't used the manual since at least 1972, and the price-fixing practice had ceased with the use of the manual.

The hearings in Washington were quite interesting. The FTC made a big deal out of the odds that any distributor would get to high levels with Amway, as though that were of vital importance. Of course, we publish those figures now for everyone to see, and they don't seem to have made a dent in our distributor force. During Rich's testimony on the stand, they asked him if he ever said a distributor could make $1,000 a month or that there were distributors making $50,000 a year (which was a lot of money in the 1970s). "Yes, I've said that," said Rich.

"Well, we have it on tape," the FTC fellow replied.

"That's no secret," Rich responded. "We put the tape out. I'm not going to argue that point. What's the problem?"

"A lot of people never make that amount, you know," said the FTC.

"I understand," Rich said. "I never promised it to them."

"Well, let us show you some of the people that have been hurt by this," said the FTC. And they proceeded to parade a group of people before the court. Several of them complained that they were misled by our presentation of the Amway opportunity. "I got in Amway and I worked at it for a few months but I couldn't get anybody to come to a meeting and I didn't sell any products," one fellow would say. So our lawyer would talk with him a little bit and discover that no, he'd never gone out and sold a customer on the products; no, he'd not tried very hard to get people to a meeting; and no, he'd not taken advantage of the training that his sponsors could provide.

We would often find out that even though the individual had abandoned his Amway business, he had benefited greatly from the experience. "What were you doing before you started your Amway business?" we would ask.

"I was a forklift operator at a warehouse," he would respond.

"And what are you doing now?" we would continue.

"Well, I'm selling insurance and I'm doing very well for myself."

"How did you make that transition, from forklift operator to insurance salesman?" we would press.

"Oh, everything I learned in Amway I applied to my new job."

"Thank you, sir," we would say. "Next witness!"

We were able to show the court that even these disgruntled Amway dropouts had learned so much from Amway that they'd gone on to better jobs and were far more successful than they had been before Amway.

VINDICATED

After four years of legal proceedings, literally tens of thousands of documents, hundreds of interviews, and a cost of over $4 million, the FTC upheld the Amway Sales and Marketing Plan. Commissioner Robert Pitofsky, in rendering the unanimous opinion, wrote that "we have determined that the Amway Sales and Marketing Plan is not an illegal 'pyramid scheme'; that the non-price-related rules Amway has imposed on the distributors of its products, to control the way the products flow to consumers, do not constitute unreasonable restraints of trade or unfair methods of competition; and that, with the exception of certain earnings claims, respondents [Amway] have not made false, misleading, or deceptive claims about Amway's business or the opportunities it presents to a person who becomes a part of it."

We were required to change our pricing practices and to alter the way we represented earnings to prospective distributors. Of course we were willing to abide by the judgment of the FTC, but I personally felt it to be another attack on the free-enterprise system. The freedom to contract is an essential part of a free market. Without it, business is seriously hampered in its ability to make its customers, employees, and owners better off. This country was founded upon the idea that two people ought to be able to write a contract of nearly any type and follow its terms without interference from the government. If, then, a condition of holding a distributorship or franchise or the like is to sell products at a certain price, no one is being defrauded, cheated, or robbed, and the contract should be allowed to stand.

The FTC's deputy director of information, Ira Furman, didn't see it that way. "Are we inhibiting free enterprise by stopping price-fixing?" he asked.

"We're enabling the free-enterprise system to work. We're almost a deregulatory agency—we deregulate the effects of businesses regulating other businesses."

This would be really funny if it were not for the fact that such "deregulation" results in incalculable injury to the economy each year. As long as the contracts between businesses are freely entered into, without guise or fraud, business "regulation," as Mr. Furman thinks of it, is very different from government regulation. The business relationships or agreements the FTC prosecutes are voluntary. Free people typically only enter into contracts they believe will be beneficial to them. Government regulation is not a contract. Bureaucrats make the rules and businesses have to follow them. There is nothing voluntary, nothing beneficial, about government regulation.

If we were disappointed by the ruling on price-fixing, we were relieved that the FTC perceived the fairness and necessity of our rule prohibiting distributors from selling to retail stores. The essence of the Amway organization is person-to-person selling. Individuals selling to their friends, relatives, and neighbors can provide much better service than a retail store. The restriction, then, was a commonsense way to assure the customer of excellent service.

With regard to earnings claims, the judgment the FTC rendered must be understood in the context of their peculiar legal understanding of "deception." At the time of the judgment, Rich told the press, "Significantly, the commission did not find even one instance where a prospective distributor was misled by examples of how our Sales and Marketing Plan works. Instead, the commission chose to base its conclusion on a purely theoretical legalistic standard called the capacity to deceive. That's quite a different matter. What the commission is saying is that somebody, someday, somewhere might possibly be misled." Today, the average monthly income of active distributors is clearly marked in several places on the handout issued at every presentation of the Sales and Marketing Plan.

HOW TO SPOT A PYRAMID

This wasn't the first or last time Amway would be attacked as a pyramid scheme. But this charge is absurd. First, pyramids usually require a substantial, nonrefundable entry fee. Amway's fee for the starter kit is both low and refundable. At the time of the FTC investigation, a sales kit cost $15 and a product sample kit cost $10. Further, if a new distributor wants to leave Amway, his sponsor must buy back the unused inventory.

Second, Amway thrives on sales of high-quality products. Pyramids rely exclusively on recruitment into the organization, though they will sometimes market low-quality or useless products to camouflage their activities. Though Amway distributors can multiply or enhance their business volume through recruitment, without sales, no one makes a dime through Amway. Distributors must satisfy customers in order to make the Amway Plan work. There is no payment to distributors for adding distributors to their organization.

Third, true pyramid schemes can quickly "saturate" a market, meaning that after a period of rapid growth, there's no one left to recruit and the system collapses. The FTC allegations as to saturation were ridiculous and betrayed a gross lack of understanding of how the Amway marketing plan works. After fifteen years in operation, Amway had distributors in only one quarter of 1 percent of the nation's households. Amway presents no danger of market saturation—a concept the FTC finally grasped. Today, after nearly forty years of growth, Amway still has a lot of potential. Each distributor is free to establish branches not only in his own community but worldwide. This provides an enormous population within which to work.

To keep from being duped into an illegal pyramid scheme, I encourage people to ask a few simple questions when someone presents them with a new business proposition:

1. Does the promoter make claims of very high yields on an initial investment? Claims of 1,000 percent annual returns, or higher, are not unusual in pyramid schemes.
2. Does the promoter want a high, nonrefundable entry fee?
3. Does the business sell a product or service? Is the product or service high quality?
4. Does the promoter insist on secrecy or evade legality questions?
5. Is the business a member of the Direct Selling Association? If so, that's good—the DSA has fought illegal pyramid schemes by educating the public and seeking criminal penalties for those promoting these schemes. They also maintain a code of ethics and guidelines for their members.

The FTC never challenged Amway's product quality and value. Pyramid schemes usually produce nothing—their short lives are marked by transfers of money from one person to another. Genuine businesses, in contrast, care about consumer satisfaction and manufacture good-quality products. The FTC noted, however, that "Amway's products have very high consumer acceptance. A marketing specialist . . . stated that Amway's laundry detergent, which has a very small market share and no national advertising, ranks third out of thirty-seven brands in brand loyalty. Amway's liquid dishwashing soap led all sixteen brands surveyed in brand loyalty."

After the FTC investigators left in 1979, Amway was still strong—in fact, fiscal 1979 saw retail sales of $800 million, up $300 million from the previous year. It turned out that the FTC investigation was a good thing for us in the long run. Not only did it teach us something about dealing with the government and bureaucracies, it gave us a renewed credibility that we could use later on. If someone questioned the legitimacy of the Amway Plan, we could say, "Look, the FTC had the same concerns you do. They investigated us thoroughly, and we came out okay. We're even used as a model of the right way to run a direct-selling business." When we entered foreign countries for the first time, many of them had not seen a direct-selling business like ours. We were able to allay their fears by telling them about our experiences with the FTC. If they didn't have any laws on the books to distinguish between legitimate direct sellers and unscrupulous pyramid operations, we encouraged them to use U.S. laws as a model for their own rules. In spite of all the negative publicity that arose from the FTC investigation, if we had not undergone that rigorous test, it would have been much more difficult for us to expand internationally as we have done.

In 1982 came another trial at the hands of the Wisconsin Justice Department. This was, in a sense, a less serious attack as it did not threaten the very existence of Amway. However, the publicity that resulted from the Wisconsin affair did us no service.

Amway literature handed out to prospective distributors included some hypothetical examples of what kinds of income were possible in independent Amway businesses. The state of Wisconsin insisted that the statements Amway made were improper and sued Amway and four Wisconsin distributors. We contended that our figures should stand as we stated them.

As with all other legitimate forms of self-employment, income from an Amway business depends upon the individual effort devoted to building that business plus the time spent. Some people enter Amway as solely a part-time occupation— something to bring in a little extra cash every month. Others sought to use the Amway opportunity to its maximum potential and work at it full-time. Also, distributors in the early stages of building their businesses cannot expect to receive what the senior distributors upline from them are making. And then there are distributors like the one who tried to start his Amway business by purchasing thousands of dollars of audiovisual equipment with which to impress those at his sales meetings (maybe he thought that if he spent enough, he wouldn't have to work). All these factors mean that the average distributorship is not generating the kind of income that is possible with Amway. Our sales literature, however, in its hypothetical examples, presented the kind of income a hardworking individual who has spent several years in the business could receive.

MAKING IT BIG IN AMWAY

Some people fail to realize that Amway is not, and has never been, a get-rich-quick scheme. Some Amway distributors have become very wealthy in a short span of time. This isn't always the case, however. Most people who want to take their businesses to their greatest potential will have to do what Rich and I did when we were starting out—work long hours without quitting too easily. We realized, through our experiences with the media, that we would have to make that crystal-clear to people. The "Amway Business Review," which distributors hand out at all presentations of the Amway Sales and Marketing Plan, now includes information on average monthly income and bonuses for our distributors.

Many of our Amway distributor meetings and rallies feature distributors who have made it big—people who are making six-figure incomes through Amway. But to look only at these success stories is to miss the really big success story—the millions of people all over the world who have a little better piece of life's goodness today because they put some of their spare time every week into Amway. In upstate New York, the mother who needs that little extra to help send her children to a parochial school and wants to work from her home. In Turkey, the father of six children who has an Amway distributorship just to buy groceries for his large family. In Japan, the businessman who sells Amway products to pay for vacations in Hawaii. Maybe they're only putting in five hours a week because their goal is just to have a little extra spending money. Maybe they're putting in ten to help send a child off to college. The opportunity is there, and each Amway distributor has decided for himself how far he's going to take it. We said, "Listen, here's the deal. We've set this up so that you can make of it what you want. Don't tell us about your troubles. Don't tell us what you can't do. Just take this opportunity and show us what you can do with it."

We can't make the plan absolutely foolproof. Any business undertaking involves some risk, though we've worked to reduce that risk to an absolute minimum. We can't completely monitor, much less control, the behavior of millions of distributors to make sure that a few unscrupulous people aren't misrepresenting the Amway Plan or to keep people from making poor decisions with their businesses. But Rich and I are convinced that our plan works well for most people. It has stood the test of time. We're willing to defend it against those who can't stand to watch others succeed.

Yet these early challenges to our business practices drove home to Rich and me the importance of understanding and participating in the political process. Government officials who did not understand multilevel marketing had the power to shut us down with a court case or new regulations. Nowhere was this more true than what was about to happen in Canada.

CHAPTER 8

Hamstrung in Canada

On November 12, 1982, the Royal Canadian Mounted Police raided Amway's Canadian headquarters. In a twenty-minute statement to the press, a spokesman for the Canadian government laid criminal charges against Amway, claiming that Amway had "defrauded" Revenue Canada of an undetermined sum in excess of $28 million. Revenue Canada, the Canadian equivalent of the IRS, sued Amway in the largest customs lawsuit it had ever filed, seeking $118 million (US) in back duty and penalties. In addition, Rich and I, along with two of our vice presidents, were threatened with extradition to stand trial in a Canadian court. With that day came the climax of the worst ordeal Amway ever faced, and an unrivaled publicity nightmare.

The day after the Canadian press conference we held a press conference of our own in Ada. Rich and I, and our two accused vice presidents, explained our side of the story to the press. Most of the problems, we were having to deal with had their root in 1965, when the relationship between Canada and the United States was somewhat more friendly than it was in 1982. To understand what was really going on in 1982, something of an explanation of the history of our dealings with Canada is necessary.

Canadian customs law placed tariffs on imported items based on their fair market valuation in the country of origin. Amway's unique organizational structure meant that the system would have to be adapted for our situation. So in 1965, we sat down with Canadian customs officials to develop a customs ruling regarding Amway products produced in the United States and exported to Canada. Amway would pay the same tariff that (1) its competitors selling to stores paid; (2) Amway would have paid if it had brought the products from other manufacturers; or (3) Amway would have paid if it had sold the products to non-Amway outlets in the United States. In August of 1965, that ruling was made by Canadian customs officials. For fifteen years, from 1965 to 1980, both the Canadian government and Amway observed this fair and equitable ruling.

During this time, Canadian customs officials routinely audited the valuation methods Amway used for products it shipped to Amway of Canada. Each time, Canadian customs officials indicated their satisfaction with the arrangements, which met terms of the 1965 agreement. Then, in early 1980, Canadian customs unilaterally changed the 1965 ruling. Amway was required to pay over four times the tariff it paid between 1965 and 1980 on the very same products.

Why the sudden change?

An Amway executive who had been in our employ for only about two years took it upon himself to challenge the 1965 ruling made by Canadian customs officials. Even though he had not been personally involved in the 1965 negotiations and was uninformed as to the basis of the ruling, he prodded our auditing firm and our Canadian customs broker (neither of whom were involved in the 1965 discussions) into believing that fraudulent misrepresentations had been made in 1965 and during subsequent audits. He even attempted to convince Rich and me that a fraud had been committed. This was disturbing to us, of course, and we promptly looked into his allegations, relying upon legal counsel from inside and outside Amway. When we decided not to adopt his recommendation to pay Revenue Canada the sum he said we owed, he resigned.

He had been skillful in his presentation to the customs broker, however, and the broker soon resigned as Amway's representative. Without fully investigating the executive's allegations, the broker sent a letter to Revenue Canada relating what he had said. So in a strange way, Amway blew the whistle on itself, though no foul had actually been committed. Revenue Canada then issued its 1980 ruling.

Obviously, at this point we were very concerned. The new ruling was tantamount to stopping us from shipping goods to Canada. But more important, the integrity of the company was placed in doubt. We resorted once more to outside advice to determine the rightness of the situation.

Amway hired Vernon D. Acree, retired U.S. commissioner of customs, as a customs consultant to review the tariff arrangement. Acree determined that there were no facts to support a charge of concealment, cover-up, or fraud. He reported that he did not find in his review of memos or from numerous interviews and other investigations any instance where anyone from Amway had defrauded the Canadian government. "The Canadians seem to have come on rather heavy-handed in this situation," Acree said. "You don't bring criminal charges without examining the other side of the coin. No one from Canada has been to Ada to say, 'Here are the allegations. What is your response?'"

Heavy-handed, indeed. So severe was the response from Revenue Canada that we began to suspect that the animosity Canadian prime minister Pierre Trudeau had toward business, and American business in particular, might be filtering through to this situation. Maybe Trudeau's leftist government had taken offense to our conservatism. The Canadian journalist Bruce LaPlaunte noted that the sweet smell of successful capitalism may have been odoriferous to Trudeau and his Liberal Party. "Some Amway people are, dare I say it, VERY successful," LaPlaunte wrote. "Guess what political-philosophical system most (if not all) of them espouse? Capitalism. What is the basic tenet of capitalism? That given a modicum of freedom one can accomplish just about anything one wants to accomplish. And what does Amway preach? That given a reasonable amount of effort, one can make a very nice living being an Amway rep." Trudeau, a man Ed Feulner described as a "devotee of socialist economics" who "winces when he hears free-market success stories," was facing a tough election battle with the very conservative Peter Pocklington. Pocklington, a businessman from the Calgary-Edmonton area, was a favorite of some of our Canadian distributors. He was invited to some of the big Amway functions, became quite popular, and for a while it appeared that Pocklington was going to defeat Trudeau. All of a sudden some strange things started to happen. Amway trucks were stopped at the border for long periods of time. Distributors started getting all kinds of audits. Other American firms began experiencing similar problems. The war Trudeau's bureaucrats were waging on American business may have been a mistake, given the number of Canadians buying American imports and making money from American investment.

Amway gets audited throughout the world and has had no significant importing problems anywhere but Canada. We export half a billion dollars' worth of goods to Japan each year. We get audited there on a regular basis and we've never had a problem. During the entire Revenue Canada debacle, we were exporting at the exact same price to a variety of other markets. That we continued to export with consistent pricing elsewhere indicates that Canada was out of step with the world trade protocol. Canada used a one-of-a-kind import valuation method employed by no other nation and had an antiquated, senseless set of import restrictions. Ironically, after our confrontation with Revenue Canada, Canada changed its protocol. Under current trade regulations, the export pricing system we used would not even be questioned.

NOT ALONE

Amway wasn't Revenue Canada's only target. Canadian firms had been getting worked over by Revenue Canada for years. The Canadian Organization of Small Business complained bitterly, "No matter how orderly our tax affairs may be, Revenue Canada can always find a way to destroy us."

While it may be said that Revenue Canada received lower customs duties than it might have without the 1965 ruling, Amway Canada nevertheless paid over $23 million in Canadian customs duties before the rules were changed. During the same period, Amway paid nearly $5 million more in Canadian federal sales tax assessments. Additionally, Amway of Canada, Ltd., grew into a company doing over $100 million a year in business, employing (directly or indirectly) thousands of Canadians and servicing 100,000 Canadian distributorships, which represented perhaps 150,000 to 200,000 people. Amway of Canada paid millions upon millions of dollars in income taxes. Amway's purchases of products and services from Canadian companies added another immeasurable benefit to the Canadian economy.

Revenue Canada managed to hit us hard financially, even without the taxes. The bad publicity and the recession contributed to a significant fall in U.S. sales during 1982. Our international expansion really paid off, balancing out domestic shortfalls and allowing us to finish the year with a small increase in sales, up to $1.5 billion from $1.4 billion in 1981. Some months, though, we were actually losing money, and earnings went to almost nothing. If Amway had been a publicly held company, our stock values would have plunged. Revenue Canada and the state of Wisconsin took their toll—nothing before or since has hurt Amway so badly.

During the entire Revenue Canada episode, our distributors were faithful to Amway, rallying around the company just as we expected they would. Supportive letters and phone calls from distributors, friends, suppliers, and customers poured into corporate headquarters in Ada. One such communication was a telegram from Vancouver, British Columbia, simply stating, "We're behind you all the way." It was signed by 209 distributors! Amway had provided millions of people with an opportunity to enjoy financial independence and success through their Amway businesses. Now these grateful people repaid us with phenomenal loyalty.

Our employees stood behind us as well. One of them, signing himself "A Faithful Amway Employee," wrote Rich and me an encouraging letter early in 1983:

> I know how positive you always have to sound when up in front of the people—I also know how wearing this whole ordeal with Canada and with the downtrend of U.S. sales has been on you—it shows, and I also can see how hard it is for you to be positive, when reality seems so stark. You've spent years and years telling people how great we are, and making them believe it—now it's time for you to really believe it yourself. Everyone in every facet of

life makes mistakes—sure Amway has made some, but they weren't intentional—we here at World Headquarters have always tried to do what was best—we haven't always been successful, but the effort was true, the intention was good—and good will always prevail. This transitional period is merely a trying time, if you will, a test of our faith, yours and mine. Don't give up the faith! That's what it's all about, you know.

When I think about the teamwork, selflessness, and unity our distributors and employees demonstrated, I'm reminded of an analogy from the animal kingdom. When geese fly south this winter in the familiar "V" formation, consider what scientists have discovered about why they fly that way.

As each bird flaps its wings, it creates an uplift for the bird immediately following. By flying in V formation, the whole flock adds at least 71 percent greater flying range than if each bird flew on its own.

Point: People who share a common direction and sense of community can get where they are going more quickly and easily because they are traveling on the trust of one another.

When a goose falls out of formation, it suddenly feels the drag and resistance of trying to go it alone and quickly gets back into formation to take advantage of the lifting power of the bird in front. When the head goose gets tired, it rotates back in the "V," and another goose leads.

Point: It is sensible to take turns doing demanding jobs with people.

Finally, when a goose gets sick or is wounded by gunshot and falls out of formation, two other geese fall out with that goose and follow it down to lend help and protection. They stay with the fallen goose until it is able to fly or until it dies; and only then do they launch out, on their own or with another formation, to catch up with their group.

Point: If we have the sense of a goose, we will stand by each other like that! We all need to be reminded of these basic truths when troubles come. When Revenue Canada threatened us, Rich and I had to remember to stand by each other and provide help when it's needed, and to encourage distributors and employees to do the same.

Amway was not alone in its defense against Revenue Canada—we received the help and encouragement of several prominent political figures. Two Michigan congressmen, Guy VanderJagt and Harold Sawyer, spoke up in support of Amway on the floor of the U.S. House of Representatives. VanderJagt condemned Revenue Canada's tactics, saying that "we do not seek a world trade war, but enough is enough. Amway does not intend to be a 'fall guy' to the Canadian government. I applaud them for sticking to their guns. The most sad commentary on the whole situation, however, is the time, the effort, and undoubtedly huge sums of money that now must be expended by Amway in its 'truth campaign' to prove its innocence and demonstrate the absurdity of the Canadian charges."

Despite the wonderful support we received, our defense was not going well. Hampering our efforts to defend ourselves was an increasingly disorganized legal team. By the end of 1982 we had ten law firms working on the case as well as an outside legal coordinator. We couldn't get a straight answer out of any of the lawyers, and they were costing us a fortune. Someone from the outside needed to come in and straighten out the problem. So in December of 1982, I called my old friend Bill Nicholson, who had been a White House aide to President Ford. He had followed the situation through newspapers and magazines and was willing to come up and help us out just as a favor.

Bill arrived in January and discovered pretty quickly that our legal coordinator was at the heart of the problem. He had forced all ten law firms to clear everything through him so that no one knew the whole picture and had done other things that complicated matters immensely.

Confusing matters further was the fight with the Canadian government on two levels. Because the civil case that Revenue Canada had against us didn't allow for extradition, the Canadians had to come at us from the provincial level with a criminal suit in order to threaten us with extradition and really put pressure on us.

In early July 1983, Bill met with the Canadian attorney general and made a breakthrough in the provincial case. As a result, the criminal charges against Rich and me were dropped after Amway paid a $21 million (US) fine to the province of Ontario in October. Paying the fine was not something that we wanted to do initially. The fine was a substantial one. We felt, however, that in order to put the issue behind us and get on with our lives, it would be best to pay. The headlines were hurting us, and the longer the case was in the courts, the more headlines we would see. If we had stayed in the fight long enough, we would have lost by winning!

SETTLING THE ISSUE

In September 1989, after six more years of legal wrangling and posturing over the civil case, we decided it would be best to negotiate a settlement with Revenue Canada. Again, this was distasteful to me, but the alternative was another eight to ten years of dragging the case through the courts. The Canadian authorities realized, I think, that we were ready to walk away from our Canadian assets if we could not come to terms on the issue. We had only two facilities in Canada in 1989, worth less than 10 percent of the amount Revenue Canada had been seeking.

It was not as though the $38 million settlement would hurt Amway—we completed the 1989 fiscal year with sales of $1.9

billion and were in a very strong financial position. And leaving our Canadian assets behind would have been less expensive, in one sense. Over one hundred thousand Canadian distributors and hundreds of employees, however, were depending on Amway. To cut our ties to Canada and leave them unsupported or unemployed would hurt them and make a statement about Amway's dealings with distributors, employees, and customers that we didn't want to make.

During the Revenue Canada issue, we brought General Alexander Haig to Amway as a consultant for international affairs. It was at a Heritage Foundation board meeting in the late 1970s that I got to know Al, and he soon became a close personal friend of mine. When Revenue Canada started coming after us, we knew that we needed help. Al had started his own consulting business after leaving government service, and his experience in touchy international situations was invaluable. We didn't want the press to know at the time that he was consulting with us—Al was a high-profile figure and we didn't want the attention his involvement might bring. Of course, Al had been giving speeches at our conventions for some time, but if people discovered that he was doing more than that, it could have raised some eyebrows. So we had to whisk him in and out of Grand Rapids secretly and keep him out of the view of the public. On most of his visits, Al stayed at Rich's guest house.

Morale had suffered somewhat overseas during our preoccupation with Revenue Canada, so we enlisted Al to go around on our behalf to Great Britain, France, and Germany to meet with distributors, make assessments, and generally let them know that we hadn't forgotten about them. Al is highly respected in Europe, and his presence had a powerful effect on Amway's progress there. Both domestically and internationally, sales growth began to pick up again.

Al definitely had experience in managing tough situations, and he had unmatched leadership talent. As chief of staff under

President Nixon, Alexander Haig was virtually functioning as president of the country during the last days before Nixon's resignation. He had a good handle on what should be done and the ability to get it accomplished.

Al had developed a close working relationship with Prime Minister Trudeau while working under President Nixon. While Al certainly didn't see eye to eye with Trudeau on political issues, he was expert at keeping the peace between the two governments. Richard Nixon didn't care much for Trudeau, so Al had to be the intermediary for a lot of official state business. Al's personal contacts and ability to communicate effectively with the Canadian government helped us immensely.

Under the stress and pressure of the Canadian charges and the negative publicity they generated, it would have been easy for Rich and me to begin blaming each other for Amway's problems during the Canadian crisis. Instead of standing back to back, fending off attacks, we could have turned against one another. To avoid tension between us, we drew on our forty-year friendship and our old habits of working things out peacefully. If we had resorted to tearing each other down, we would have destroyed everything we had built in all our years together. Rich is a terrific business partner, and I wouldn't have made it through the Canada crisis without his encouragement, wisdom, and support. Just as Rich and I depended on one another through everything, Amway's survival during this time depended upon the strength of our friendship. Our assailants would have won if they had managed to drive the two of us apart.

The Revenue Canada crisis came close to throwing Amway off track as a company. After years of legal battles, we were in danger of losing our focus on the business, of forgetting why we started Amway in the first place. There was a kind of arteriosclerosis, a hardening of the arteries, that had developed within the corporate structure. Most companies go through this process after they've matured, and if they fail to deal with the problem, younger, more vibrant competing firms are ready to step in to take their place.

CHANGES AT THE TOP

The Revenue Canada crisis also showed us that we needed to replace our outside legal coordinator and perhaps a few other top-level executives. We had several senior executives who seemed to be forgetting the big picture. Their efficiency was not what it could have been, and neither were our profit margins. While they conducted endless meetings, Rich and I watched Amway's growth numbers become smaller and smaller. The whole situation was really distressing, but neither Rich nor I had the heart to make all the changes ourselves. Once again, we turned to our friend Bill Nicholson. We asked Bill if he would come up and do some surgery on Amway. "Okay," Bill agreed. "I'll try to make sense out of it and I'll come in for a few months. Here's what I want to do. I'm going to stop in next week on my way back from Germany. I'll be in on Thursday night. On Friday, I'm going to terminate your outside legal coordinator and then I'll go back to Houston over the weekend. I'll get some winter clothes. I'll be back up to start bright and early Monday morning."

So that Monday, the 5th of March, 1984, we laid out the whole Amway structure on a big sheet of butcher paper and started in. The next few months marked a turnaround for Amway. As hard as it was to make the needed changes, it paid off. Our rate of growth picked back up and showed no signs of slowing down. Instead of leveling off as a "middle-aged" twenty-five-year-old company, Amway had entered a second era of growth and development.

THE PROBLEM OF PROTECTIONISM

The problems we had with Revenue Canada illustrated to me all too clearly the problems that result from trade restrictions. Despite the difficulties that Amway and other companies have faced when marketing overseas, I strongly feel that free foreign trade is vital for promoting a high standard of living and world peace. History shows that the world has been more peaceful when there is free trade than when there is restricted trade. Trade wars tend to escalate to hot wars. Some people believe that World War II was brought on in part by the extremely high Smoot-Hawley tariffs of the depression years. That may or may not be true, but it is clear that the costs of protectionism outweigh the benefits. This is why, in my first speech for the U.S. Chamber of Commerce, I advocated a free-trade agreement for North America—a plan that later became accepted as NAFTA.

Calls for trade restrictions to protect this or that industry from foreign competition are misguided. The protected industry may benefit for a while, but in the long run it will become incompetent, unable to sell its products overseas. Furthermore, domestic customers pay higher prices for those products.

Amway has benefited tremendously from foreign trade, as have thousands of other firms. In a freer trading system, Amway and other international companies will continue to flourish. While artificial trade barriers allow firms to become fat and sloppy, free trade promotes efficiency in domestic firms and the well-being of consumers.

Freedom is not without its problems, however, as I learned in my dealings with our nation's free press. And while I support the concept of freedom of the press, the way some media interpret it made life miserable for us for a while.

CHAPTER 9

In the Limelight

With the Revenue Canada dispute came a whole year of publicity problems for Amway. Newspapers and television shows, most with a decidedly liberal bent, used our problems with the Canadian tax authorities as a springboard for all manner of unjustified criticisms.

A hailstorm of serious attacks came as a series of stories in the *Detroit Free Press* in the fall of 1982. With the August headline "Amway's Plot to Bilk Canada of Millions" and a story on "the Amway scheme," the left-leaning paper engaged in a war against us. In October, another series tried to brand Amway as a cultic pyramid scheme. The behavior of some star distributors was taken out of context and ridiculed. Amway dropouts with family or financial problems were sought out and their troubles blamed on Amway. Never mind that the FTC had ruled that Amway was not an illegal pyramid scheme. Never mind the thousands of ordinary people who gained family unity and enjoyed success through Amway. Those stories don't sell newspapers nearly as well as the ones tearing down prosperous businesses.

With any large organization like Amway's, there are those who have negative experiences and leave with a bad impression of the whole organization. While we can work to reduce those occurrences, they cannot be eliminated altogether. And there are certainly those distributors, even at high levels, who will say and do things that are improper. With millions of distributors worldwide, it is difficult to keep all of them in line. Because of the structure of the Amway organization, the influence the corporate leadership has over distributors must be predominantly indirect. Amway distributors are not employees. They are owners of independent businesses who are linked with each other by a common set of products, a system of bonuses, and a zeal for free enterprise.

Clearly, ideological differences were affecting the press's journalism. An earlier, front-page article in the June 15, 1980, *Detroit Free Press* described me as "the acknowledged financial wizard of Amway," "the serious one of the two, the angry one with the computer mind and alarming speeches about the destructive forces of a meddling 'central government.'" I didn't realize I was such a troll. I must admit that the speeches would be alarming, but only to someone who thinks that government is too small, too weak, and too unobtrusive.

Obviously, our company was being attacked because we were an outstanding example of what free enterprise can do when allowed to work. The *Free Press* stories reeked of political smear tactics. Rich and I took the offensive. We cleared out an old boardroom and began using it as a crisis management center. Equipped with telephones and fax machines and dubbed "the War Room," it was staffed around the clock as we sought to counter the publicity crisis sparked by the Revenue Canada issue. We launched a "truth campaign" in an effort to counteract the multiple accusations being made against us. From the deck of my summer home, I would write the copy of full-page ads that we placed in American and Canadian newspapers to get the truth out.

The years 1982–1985 were a very trying time for me. I felt the need to take control of the situation, but control seemed to be in the hands of the major media. There was a very adversarial feeling between ourselves and the media early on, during the first publicity crises. Rich and I both were incensed at first, then frustrated by the power newspapers and television had over the American public. The newspapers and television had the ability to define us for the public—to present a false image of what we were all about at Amway. Revenue Canada provided anti-free-enterprise newspaper editors and television producers an opportunity to make their views clear while tearing down two men who held opinions different from their own. At times, we felt almost completely helpless. What does one do when the press is wildly off target with a story? How does one correct the negative public perceptions that are generated by a series of wrongheaded articles? I could write a letter to the editor, which they may or may not print, seven days later, in a much less prominent place than where the story first appeared. The attempts we did make to correct the story through counteradvertising were expensive and not nearly as effective as a couple of front-page articles in a major newspaper would have been. We are at a definite disadvantage when we don't have the access to people's eyes and ears that the major media has. Network marketing firms like Amway also suffer from a media bias against them, simply because network marketing firms rarely advertise in the mainstream media. While newspapers and other media may be threatened with the loss of billions of advertising dollars if they go after traditional firms with sensationalistic reporting, they have less to lose by targeting firms like Amway.

Our "truth campaign" was necessarily limited in its success simply because advertising can't compete with front-page news stories. One of the few options left to us was a lawsuit against the *Detroit Free Press*. This was a risky strategy because the paper could always use the suit against us by presenting it as a crazy, unfounded action. "What, don't you believe in the freedom of the press?" they might say. Of course we do, but when that freedom is used to cause immeasurable and unjustified damage to the reputation of individuals and firms, we believe that a lawsuit is an appropriate legal recourse. So we threatened the *Detroit Free Press* with a $500 million lawsuit (which we later dropped because it might have affected the ongoing court case with Revenue Canada), and Rich even ordered the *Detroit Free Press* to be taken out of the Amway Grand Plaza Hotel. The problems we faced in those years alerted us to the importance of the media and its ability to affect public opinion. In the interest of liberty, we need to preserve the freedom of the press, but the press should commit to using its power responsibly. Rather than pump out sensationalism and tabloid-style stories, the media needs to report what's really news, truthfully. If journalists, editors, and news anchors demonstrate honesty and self-restraint, the American people will continue to trust the media.

A BALANCED *60 MINUTES*

On January 9, 1983, we faced the possibility of even more publicity problems. That was the Sunday night that the TV show *60 Minutes* was to air "Soap and Hope," a segment devoted to Amway. We weren't sure what to expect, but we were pretty happy with the way things turned out. The show's portrayal of Amway was fair and balanced. We set out to cooperate from the very beginning, and we think this helped us to some extent.

Rich and I were both interviewed by Mike Wallace for the

show, as were several disgruntled former Amway distributors. We were wary of Mike's interviewing tactics, however, and we made sure that we were well prepared for his visits. We got Walter Pfister, a former ABC vice president, to train us for an interview situation. "If Amway people don't do their own talking," Wally said, "somebody else will do it for them. . . . My feeling is that if the company has nothing to hide . . . and has articulate spokespersons, then do it!" Many executives are caught off guard by skillful interviewers, and their fumbling or defensive responses can make a poor impression on the television audience. So Wally and his Executive Television Workshop in New York made sure we were ready. Aware of the possible negative outcome, however, we made sure that an Amway camera taped the interview too. If the CBS editors skewed things in a misleading direction, we'd be sure to know about it. Tagging along behind the *60 Minutes* crew on their tour of our Ada facilities was another camera, filming what CBS filmed. Not everything the segment showed was positive—in fact, there was enough negative in it to upset quite a few distributors.

Given Mike Wallace's reputation, however, we were pleased to have come out looking so good. It used to be said that "you know it's going to be a bad day when you arrive at your office and find Mike Wallace and a *60 Minutes* crew there waiting for you." After his visit, however, he was able to tell reporters, talk-show hosts, and others that his "preconceived misconceptions" about Amway were untrue. "We found [Amway's] products are good, and that they're not a pyramid operation," he told one reporter. To Ted Koppel, Wallace said,

I think a business serves itself much better by being forthcoming, by taking its chances unless it has something to hide. . . . Let me give you examples. The Amway Corporation . . . felt they had something to gain by making the best case that they could. They didn't ask for questions ahead of time, they didn't ask for any special editing privileges. They were forthcoming, they opened their books, they opened their plants to us. And as a result, you can talk to these people, and they'll say, perhaps it wasn't the broadcast that we would have liked to see, but it was fair, it was balanced, it was accurate, and we probably did ourselves good in the long run.

SANDBAGGED BY DONAHUE

Unfortunately, not everyone in the media has Mike Wallace's fairness. We found that out the hard way on April 20, 1983, when Rich was interviewed on the *Phil Donahue Show*. (Does anyone remember him anymore?) What we thought would be an opportunity to counter some of the negative media reports of recent months turned into a free-for-all against Amway. I had elected not to appear on the Donahue show, and had encouraged Rich not to appear. In my opinion, Donahue and people like him are not after the truth—they're after something with which to entertain their listeners, and the entertainment is often at the expense of the guest on the show. By participating I felt that we were setting ourselves up for some bad publicity. Rich believed that he should make an appearance, however. Donahue would produce the show with or without us, Rich said, and we would at least be able to defend ourselves if one of us appeared on the show.

We were aware that the show would review the complaints of some former Amway distributors who felt that the Amway opportunity had been misrepresented to them. Rich had agreed to appear on the condition that he be allowed to state our position during a five- to ten-minute one-on-one interview with Donahue before going to the audience. This was the usual format for Donahue's show, and we didn't anticipate any problems. During the interview, Rich was to freely admit that there had been some distributors who had violated our rules of conduct, and then explain that we had a solution. We had set up a ten-point program to correct misleading representations among our distributors—from extensive counseling to outright termination of a distributorship in some situations.

Instead of abiding by our agreement, Donahue blindsided us. After showing a film clip of one of our rallies from the *60 Minutes* show, he skipped the preliminary interview entirely and went straight to the audience. Rich was positioned in the middle of the stage, with a group of Amway distributors on his right and a group of disgruntled former Amway distributors on his left. What could have been an intelligent discussion soon turned into a circus, as Donahue allowed the anti-Amway side of the audience to interrupt and shout down Rich repeatedly. Donahue and his producers, we discovered later, had coached the anti-Amway side beforehand, encouraging them to be "very, very assertive." Many times, Rich would begin a sentence, only to be rudely cut off by some former distributor who believed that Amway had somehow brought about his personal family problems or financial distress. These people quoted statistics that they would not or could not support and made wild accusations against Rich and against Amway that were totally without foundation. To make matters worse, there were five microphones active at once—one for Rich, one for Donahue, and three more for the studio and call-in audiences. Despite all of this, we concluded after the show that Amway had come out looking good simply because the anti-Amway side had behaved so poorly. Throughout the show, Rich and our Amway distributors were polite and calm, while the other side acted in a completely uncivilized manner.

William Rusher, a columnist for *National Review*, commented that Donahue "must have been having a bad day when Rich DeVos was on. . . . I have never seen a television guest more rudely trampled." The whole hourlong ordeal was a real test of

Rich's patience. He never got a chance to fully answer any of the groundless accusations thrown at him, and Donahue refused to manage the anti-Amway side so that a fair discussion could take place. Rusher said,

> DeVos sat there for an hour with a mike around his neck, doggedly trying to start a sentence in response to some question flung at him, while harridans who solemnly swore their families had been wrecked by his machinations shouted him down. Eventually, Donahue, instead of insisting that DeVos be given a chance to speak, would put him out of his misery by looking up at the overhead loudspeakers and asking "Is the caller there?"
>
> DeVos must be a cooler man than I am, because after about half an hour of that guff I would have unhooked my microphone, handed it to Donahue, told him that I would be glad to appear on his show any day he had time for me and left.

There were some courageous people who called in to the show to back Rich up. Some told how Amway had provided for their families during hard times. Others emphasized the necessity for hard work to succeed, a concept that many of the former Amway distributors had failed to grasp. "I was ten years in corporate America," one caller said. "Every weekly management meeting I went to, they said, 'Work hard and you will succeed.' Every business in America tells their new people the same thing. I feel Amway is taking the heat unjustly, because they come out publicly with their rallies and say 'Work hard and you will succeed.'"

Many people thought that Rich did very well on Donahue, despite the persecution of the anti-Amway group and Donahue's tacit acceptance of their rude behavior. Barbara Bush wrote Rich a little postcard afterwards that said "DeVos–10, Donahue–0! Love, Barbara." People who understand what we're trying to do with the Amway concept don't pay any attention to unfounded criticisms.

WAKE-UP CALLS

All of these events in the early eighties forced us to back up and give the business a careful review. They were wake-up calls, in a sense. It is easy to forget how we look from the world's perspective, and the Revenue Canada issue, the criticism (however unwarranted or unfair) in the press, and the other publicity problems helped Rich and me to see how Amway appeared to others. As Rich put it, 1982 "helped us see some of our warts." There is always room for improvement, and we recognized several areas where Amway could be doing a better job.

I think the negative media publicity took Amway out of the closet. Amway was big and visible, and we could no longer count on a low profile to save us from media attention. As a result, we were forced to become more professional in dealing with public affairs and public relations. Revenue Canada really caught us off guard. We had no public relations agency in Canada and had not invested much time in telling the Canadian people and the Canadian government who we were and what we were doing for Canada. This hurt us badly when the headlines started bashing Amway. Not having much prior knowledge of Amway, good or bad, the public was content to accept the headlines at face value.

Rich and I took all the bad publicity very hard. Sometimes I wonder how Rich and I made it through this time. It was a time of mental and physical stress that wore me down and nearly killed Rich. I don't think either of us realized how stressful everything had been until Rich had his first bout with heart problems in 1983. The load I was bearing increased tenfold as my deep concern for Rich was added to my worries over the business. Rich's health soon returned under the care of skillful surgeons, but we watched our workload more carefully after that and delegated more responsibility to others. We were forced to realize that we couldn't personally fight the media and the Canadian tax authorities and run a multibillion-dollar business at the same time. Many business owners are not as personally attached to their businesses and would have thrown in the towel. Remaking a firm's public image in the presence of an openly hostile media is not an easy task, and Rich and I both were at the point where we could have sold out and retired. In fact, while we were still recovering from some of the media blows, a major Japanese trading company approached us with an offer for Amway. Rich and I would have received a billion dollars each, in cash. Bill Nicholson had been in New York talking to this firm for several weeks, and at length he approached us one day to get a final decision. So Rich and I knocked the offer around for a minute or two and decided, "No, Bill, we want to keep the whole thing." There are times in business to pack it in and move on to other things. Rich and I sold Wolverine Air Service after three years because we felt that the period of rapid growth was nearing a decisive end, and also because we wanted to see the world. We sold our early import business and the Stone Mill Products business because better opportunities came along. We dropped the Grand Rapids Toy Company because it was simply not doing well. It's not as though Rich and I clung to Amway just because we were reluctant to sell a business we began. Our persistence with Amway through good times and bad resulted from a faith in the basic concepts behind Amway and in the people who made those concepts work. We knew the Plan's potential, and we knew we could never, in good conscience, pick up our chips and go home. Our determination soon paid off. Amway took quite a beating from the media following our troubles with Revenue Canada, but it took only a short while before Amway came back with a surge of new growth, much of it from overseas.

CHAPTER 10

Business as a Shining Light

Back in 1965, Michigan's governor, George Romney, launched "Operation Europe," aimed at increasing Michigan's business opportunities in the European market. We really hadn't considered taking Amway international, but during Operation Europe we began to realize that our person-to-person selling strategy could be applied worldwide. So we jumped in with both feet by taking a few round-the-world trips to find new markets overseas. We looked for countries with a substantial middle class, with the purchasing power for our products. The countries also had to be politically stable, without high tax rates. We hired Austen Woods as our international manager, and along with Casey Wondergem, who is now Amway's senior public affairs officer, and Bob Hooker, we started our overseas operation in Australia and then the United Kingdom.

Amway's international expansion provided the opportunity for Rich and me to extend the principles of American-style wealth creation into other countries worldwide. We saw Amway's blossoming into a multinational corporation as something positive for both the United States and the countries with which we did business. International trade allows each country to do what it does best and share the benefits of that specialization with consumers all over the world. Benjamin Franklin wrote, "No nation was ever ruined by trade," but some nations have been ruined by not enough of it.

Multinational firms act as ambassadors of economic freedom wherever they do business. When U.S. companies share some of the benefits of American-style capitalism with consumers in other nations, an advertisement for freedom is inevitably carried along with the goods. People under authoritarian regimes can't help but appreciate economic freedom when they see the quality of consumer goods that come from free nations.

Of course, the leaders of repressive regimes recognize this fact and prevent multinational firms from doing business within their borders. Multinational firms that do manage to establish themselves in a statist country must contend with corrupt bureaucrats, heavy and inconsistent taxation, poor infrastructure, and infuriating, senseless regulations. So when Rich and I looked for countries in which to expand, we looked first at those countries that were most friendly to private enterprise. But the Amway Plan has since been remarkably successful even in authoritarian nations. Today, we are seeing great success in the People's Republic of China. As eastern Europe and the former Soviet Union continue to open their doors to foreign business, we are expanding in that direction as well. My friend Dick Lesher, past president of the U.S. Chamber of Commerce, commented that "Amway has had an impact all over the world in preaching free enterprise. They're the vanguard—as soon as the door opens a crack, they're in there. A lot of people in those countries go to work with Amway because it's the quickest way to change their standard of living."

One of the greatest barriers to success in international business is the communication gap. And there is no better vehicle to bridge the communication gap in the world than music and the arts. Rich and I firmly believe that. To support the arts is to help establish a universal language of understanding between nations. So in February of 1982 when Amway had the opportunity to sponsor a European tour of the National Symphony Orchestra of Washington, we jumped right in. The tour covered eight countries and sixteen cities and featured the fantastically skilled Russian conductor Mstislav Rostropovich. The Symphony tour was really an offshoot of the 1982 Netherlands-American Bicentennial, which I'll tell you about later.

I wanted to sponsor an art exhibit for contemporary young American artists at the Stedelijk Museum in Amsterdam. Rich, who with his wife, Helen, has been a generous supporter of the Grand Rapids Symphony, suggested Amway sponsor both art and music. So we did, and with a bon voyage from Nancy Reagan, we set off to tour Europe with the orchestra and the exhibit.

CELLIST AND FREEDOM FIGHTER

Mstislav "Slava" Rostropovich is a diminutive, balding, enthusiastic Russian, who became a very dear friend of mine during the National Symphony tour. It took a little while to get used to some of his Russian ways, though. After conducting vigorously all night in these hot European auditoriums, he would invariably come up to me and give me an energetic, sweaty bear hug and a kiss.

The performances were magnificent. There were some who did not expect this finest of cellists to conduct with such inspiration and skill, but the orchestra and the maestro were lauded with standing ovations in city after city and performed no fewer than two encores at every performance. The Netherlands-American Bicentennial concert at the Concertgebouw was extraordinary. There, the orchestra received four standing ovations, which is remarkable for the reserved Dutch, who are not known for rising out of their seats to applaud! In Vienna's splendid Musikverein-saal there was standing room only. Slava, holding his baton as if it were a cello bow in his right hand, and indicating details with his left, would interpret with fiery exuberance each movement of every symphony. The musicians surpassed themselves, following the maestro with cohesion and enthusiasm. Slava was positively brilliant, giving justice to all the beauty and excitement of great classical music.

By the time the tour got to London, however, I had almost overdone my love for classical music. Slava loved to use the same two encores, a Strauss polka arranged by Shostakovich and Gershwin's "Promenade," neither of which I enjoyed very much, and I had heard them both at least a dozen times by then. I told our Amway sponsorship coordinator, Casey Wondergem, one night in London, "If I have to go to one more concert this week I am going to go home." In between performances, I kept myself pretty busy. I met with Amway executives and distributors in Europe and maintained a tight speaking schedule. The tour was, of course, wonderful for Amway branches in Europe. If there is some return to the business in the sponsorship of cultural activities, then so much the better. Sponsoring the National Symphony Orchestra was good publicity by itself, but Slava was really a folk hero at the time, and it seemed that every reporter in each of the sixteen cities wanted to interview him. At the time, our European market was brand new and growing fast. We were able to bring in our top distributors to the concerts and to the parties that followed them. Distributor pride is very important in Europe, and we wanted to promote that as much as possible.

After the tour, we were able to persuade Slava to come out

to Ada and give the Amway employees a private cello performance. In between classical selections, Slava would discourse on the history of his beautiful cello, crafted by Antonio Stradivari in 1711. The employees loved it. Not everyone enjoys classical music, but Slava created such an appreciation in his audience that day that by the end of the performance, all were on their feet in applause.

Before Slava defected from the Soviet Union, he toured with the Moscow Philharmonic and taught at the famous Moscow Conservatory. He had award-winning talent, but his outspoken support for Soviet dissidents and his friendship with Aleksandr Solzhenitsyn brought him into the disfavor of high Soviet officials in the early 1970s. Concerts and foreign tours were canceled, recordings were discontinued, and the Soviet press, television, and radio were forbidden to publicize his work. Slava and his wife, the world-famous soprano Galina Vishnevskaya, wrote an open letter to Leonid Brezhnev denouncing this oppressive treatment and requesting permission to travel abroad for two years. In 1978, after several years abroad, the Rostropoviches were stripped of their citizenship for "acts harmful to the prestige of the USSR." When he defected, the Soviet Union lost a great conductor, cellist, and pianist. His wife defected with him and deprived the Soviets of another virtuoso. Slava's passion for freedom comes through in his conducting today. "O paradox!" wrote a French reviewer, "That Slava should have to exile himself to the other side of the world, to the banks of the Potomac, to be able to glorify the Russian spirit in perfect liberty."

After coming to the United States, Rostropovich had spoken out quite eloquently against totalitarianism. He had seen how it can destroy talent by eliminating incentives and by mismanaging the remarkable brain power that the Soviet Union had at its disposal. Whenever Slava and I would talk about liberty together, this would come out in our conversation. Only in a free society can artistic talent like Slava's come to fruition

and enrich the lives of each individual. A free-enterprise economy can generate such wealth that people can afford to buy
the work of actors, artists, musicians, and others. Talented
people who cannot find enough buyers for their work will find,
in a free economy, philanthropically minded individuals to support their work. Socialism keeps everyone (except the political
elite) at such a low standard of living that they cannot afford
to support artists. In a statist economy, this is used as an excuse
to tax the population even more so that money can be devoted
to the arts. Of course, the government has not shown itself to
be a particularly good judge of what is "good" and "bad" art,
choosing rather to throw money at anyone who carries a paint-
brush, camera, or conductor's baton. Sometimes the money
lands on someone with real talent, in which case the artist runs
the risk of becoming an uninspired dependent of the state.
More often it seems to land on people who think that anything
chaotic, blasphemous, disgusting, or violent qualifies as "art."

By supporting the National Symphony Orchestra, Amway
was acting in its role as an ambassador for free enterprise. We
hoped that everyone who sat in a European auditorium to hear
the orchestra noted two things. First, Slava Rostropovich, an
example of a man once oppressed by statism and now set free
to use his abilities to the fullest. Second, funds made possible by
the American free-enterprise system working to promote those
cultural events that make human existence more enjoyable.

ECONOMIC DIPLOMACY

Business sponsorship of ambassadorial events like the National
Symphony Orchestra tour not only promote goodwill for the
company in foreign markets but also lower resistance to free-
enterprise policies in those markets. Moreover, the events can
provide a forum for international meetings between business
and government leaders, which can lead to progress toward

peaceful relations and mutually beneficial trade agreements. And who can object to that, especially when great music is involved?

In 1992, I served as commissioner general and ambassador to the Genoa Expo, the World's Fair in Genoa, Italy, commemorating the five hundredth anniversary of Christopher Columbus's voyage to America. In the spring of 1989 Bruce Gelb of the U.S. Information Agency approached me about working closely with him on the project. He knew of my work with the Netherlands-American Bicentennial and of my friendship with the U.S. ambassador to Italy, Peter Secchia. Of course, I have always had an interest in history, and Columbus's destination—the Caribbean— has always been a favorite place of mine. So I agreed to support the expo and serve as commissioner general. As I would be going on an official foreign assignment for several months, I was also given the personal rank of ambassador. I was awarded the title "Your Excellency," which I tried out on Betty, but she didn't seem to think it fit me. (Perhaps it would have worked if I had agreed to call her "Your Ladyship"!) An ambassadorship was a job I had always desired but had never been able to take on. In 1988 President Reagan had considered me for an ambassadorship to the Caribbean (the United States maintains an embassy in Barbados to serve all the Caribbean islands). I regretfully declined because of my time constraints. After being appointed commissioner general by George Bush in August of 1989, I was sworn in—twice! The first time, it was an informal swearing-in held on the deck of my summer house on Lake Michigan. Betty and I were present, along with Bruce and Ambassador Secchia. That ceremony was just to get me officially inducted, so I could sign papers and such things. The second "swearing-in" was just a formal ceremony done mainly for the benefit of the press. The first swearing-in was much more fun. Peter presented me with an enormous official gavel, and we had a great time laughing over it and speculating about its many potential uses.

The Genoa project was a great deal of fun for me, but it was sometimes very trying working with the bureaucracy. We had John Gartland from our Washington office living and working in Italy almost full-time as deputy commissioner general. He had proven himself during the Netherlands-American Bicentennial as being the sort of man who could quickly cut through government red tape to get things done, and he gave a repeat performance on the Genoa Expo. He even kept us within our budget, a marvelous feat for a World's Fair! As the major sponsor of the United States Pavilion, Amway had a big part in the World's Fair that year, and I was very proud of the work John and others did on that project.

REWRITING HISTORY

Most of the projects, international and otherwise, that Rich and I have taken on have had a substantial educational component. Sometimes I get quite an education myself from these projects. This was certainly true with the Genoa project, which opened my eyes to a massive rewrite of history that is occurring. Much to my dismay, Columbus is being portrayed in modern history books as little more than a fifteenth-century rapist. Every evil that has happened in the New World since 1492 can be tied to Columbus, some of these writers imply. In fact, Columbus was more a benevolent missionary than anything else. The Genoans were not only motivated by a desire to open better trade routes to the East but to extend the gospel of Christ to a part of the world that had not been evangelized. Columbus himself was not only a superb navigator but a serious Christian. He was not perfect, and those who followed him were not perfect. Some committed serious crimes against the indigenous people of this continent. The ideas and the religion they introduced, however, would bring Native Americans out of the spiritual, technological, and economic cave they had been trapped in for millennia. A friend of mine invented the term "occidentiphobia" to describe the fear of Western ideas that animated the attack on Columbus. That's a pretty clever way to put it. Multiculturalists in our high schools and universities preach that no culture can be considered superior to any other. "Multiculturalism" is really a misleading term. If we could think of a word that meant "any-culture-but-Western-culture-ism" it might describe the philosophy more accurately. Despite the fierce resistance from the occidentiphobics, we must use some yardstick by which to measure various cultures. Without ignoring or rejecting the positive contributions that diverse people groups add to human knowledge and culture, we should objectively, fairly, and unabashedly critique the behavior of all societies. If we insist upon complete equality of all cultures, then we are forced to accept with indifference the mass human sacrifice of some Indian tribes, the horrific massacres perpetrated by the Mongol hordes, and the raiding, raping, and pillaging of the Viking marauders.

The understanding that humans are inherently valuable because they are made in the image of God gives us a foundation for human rights. When we think of each person as bearing the imprint of the hand of God, we conclude that murderous or savage behavior is obscene and intolerable. Comprehending man's origins should also lead us to a charitable, merciful attitude toward our neighbors, without regard for race, gender, nationality, or social status. Unfortunately, not every culture has had the same view.

VILLA TAVERNA

In 1990 Rich and I and other Michigan business leaders formed what we called the Villa Taverna Society, a fund-raising organization chaired by Rich for the purpose of refurbishing

Villa Taverna, the residence of the U.S. ambassador to Italy. The historic residence in Rome had been allowed to deteriorate over the years, and Peter Secchia, as the new ambassador, was embarrassed to entertain his Italian guests in such quarters. The building itself was magnificent, but it was in terrible disrepair. Paint and wallpaper were peeling off the walls, the carpeting was threadbare, and the wiring and plumbing needed a lot of work. The State Department had no money for the needed work, so Rich and I supported the restoration in the interest of international unity and the promotion of the American way of life. Casey Wondergem, who does a lot of Amway work with our various sponsorships and fund-raisers, did a great job as usual, and the Villa Taverna Society was able to contribute in excess of $250,000 for the project.

Rich and I spent a lot of time at Villa Taverna during the fund-raising, the Genoa Expo project, and occasionally thereafter. Peter Secchia and I have been friends since. Peter is a fellow Michiganian, whom I got to know through his close association with President Ford and the Michigan Republican Party. During the Genoa Expo '92, we became closer friends. As ambassador he would introduce my speeches, and he became emcee for several expo events. It felt strange to be writing checks to the State Department for the Villa Taverna Project and to be donating more funds to the government for the Genoa project. Peter and I think alike on many government issues, and we had complained to each other many times of the latest oppressive legislation handed down from Washington. We didn't relish the thought of sending more money to the federal government, but I thought that this Villa Taverna project was worthwhile. Diplomacy, after all, is a legitimate governmental function. "It is hard to believe that we are trying to help the government," Peter said to me once. "You in Genoa— and me in Rome. They have made it so difficult. Nevertheless, fixing up these rooms is well worth it. The next ambassador will have it made. The United States government will soon be better equipped to perform its diplomatic functions. Thanks for your help."

BACK TO THE OLD COUNTRY

All of these overseas endeavors were wonderful, but you might understand why my efforts to celebrate a Netherlands-American Bicentennial were a real highlight for me.

Early in 1980 I attended a banquet in Philadelphia where I was the recipient of an award from the Holland Society of Philadelphia. The people I talked to that night convinced me of the need for some sort of international celebration of the two hundred unbroken years of friendly relations between the United States and the Netherlands. In April of 1782, the Dutch Republic was the second nation (after France) to give diplomatic recognition to the fledgling United States. After the American War for Independence, Dutch banks lent the money needed to rebuild from the war and begin an industrial revolution. These two acts launched what has become the United States' longest unmarred, peaceful relationship with any foreign power. In honor of my Dutch ancestry and culture, I decided to help celebrate the Netherlands-American Bicentennial in whatever way I could.

The first step was to get together with J. William Middendorf II, a former U.S. ambassador to the Netherlands, and a few others and set up a private, nonprofit organization called the Netherlands-American Amity Trust. Charles Tanguy, a retired Foreign Service officer with the State Department, became its executive director. Early in 1981, we formed the Netherlands-American Bicentennial Commission. I was elected its national chairman, and then-Vice President George Bush graciously accepted our invitation to serve as honorary chairman.

Because the president was attempting to cut back on national spending, most of the money for the American festivities had to come from the private sector. Bill Middendorf, Wynant Vanderpool, Casey Wondergem, and Bill Alrich worked hard to bring in $1.2 million from private donors, proving that it doesn't take government funds to throw a good party! Generous contributions from corporations and individuals enabled us to put on an orchestra tour, a yacht race, art exhibitions, and special historical exhibits in the United States and the Netherlands.

BRUSH WITH ROYALTY

In the course of the events surrounding the Netherlands-American Bicentennial, Betty and I had the privilege to meet Her Royal Majesty Queen Beatrix of the Netherlands. The very first time we met her, she extended to us an invitation to come to the palace for tea!

A visit to the palace in The Hague would be much like a visit to the White House, I imagined, but the experience turned out to be very different from what I had expected. A White House visit entails a six-level security check and constant monitoring by the Secret Service. The Netherlands is clearly a saner place—there's nothing like the paranoia that envelops the White House. I merely walked in at an entrance off the street, into an anteroom, and there Her Highness was in the next room, waiting for me. We sat down, and I was amazed to see that she poured the tea herself—there were no butlers to wait on us. The visit was quite relaxed, more like visiting one's neighbors next door than royalty, I thought.

Though I do speak some Dutch, Her Majesty's English is excellent, and therefore we conducted our conversation in that language. We discussed the bicentennial, of course, and what Her Majesty's part would be in it. As the American chairman, I had to make the arrangements for all the events in America. My audience with Queen Beatrix was intended to persuade

Her Majesty to visit the United States as a special part of the bicentennial festivities, and I was delighted to hear her agree enthusiastically to two separate visits.

Following that first meeting with the queen were a number of social events. The first was the National Symphony Orchestra's performance in Amsterdam, at the Concertgebouw Music Hall. Knowing that I would be entering with the queen, I was worried about doing it just right. It made sense to me to let her enter while I followed, but just as we were about to make the grand entrance, she turned and said, "Now you have to go ahead of me, it's the way it has to be done." Naturally, I obeyed, but it felt awkward, since I had always been taught to let women enter a room first.

The highlights of the bicentennial year were the April and June visits to the United States by the queen and her husband, Prince Claus. Their five-day state visit in April marked the first visit to the United States by a reigning Dutch monarch in thirty years. April 21 was proclaimed Amity Day in Washington, D.C., and a daylong series of events were held to honor Dutch-American relations.

Queen Beatrix was really the one who introduced me to then-Vice President and Mrs. Bush. The queen, the prince, and Betty and I enjoyed an afternoon at the National Gallery of Art in Washington, D.C., after which we had the pleasure of spending the evening at the home of the Bushes. The dinner was exquisite, as one would expect when a vice president is entertaining royalty. In honor of Her Majesty Queen Beatrix, the red, white, and blue bars of the Dutch flag of the Netherlands stood alongside the red, white, and blue of the American flags at each door.

The royal family of the Netherlands was the first royal family with whom I enjoyed a close relationship, though I had the pleasure during the National Symphony Orchestra tour to meet the king of Belgium and some of the British royal family. Each time we Americans met "Queen Bee" (as some of us came to call her), our admiration and love for her continued to grow. We admired her kind smile, her boundless energy, her warm but businesslike manner, and her large collection of hats!

I learned, however, that being around royalty puts you in line for the kind of tabloid treatment they deal with all the time. One morning my assistant handed me a copy of a Belgian "newspaper" with a huge picture of Her Majesty and me aboard our airplane with a headline, in French, that said something like "American Millionaire Woos Queen Beatrix." Inside were more photos and captions showing me entering and leaving The Hague with the queen and of Her Majesty at the reception in Grand Rapids. The attempt to link us romantically gave all of us but Betty quite a laugh. She felt better later when the queen told her that no one in the Netherlands takes those tabloids seriously.

The real fun began with the June royal visit by the royal couple. For two weeks the queen and her husband toured the United States coast to coast. My favorite part, of course, was her appearance in Grand Rapids. Grand Rapids and the neighboring town of Holland had a whole day of festivities planned, and Gerald Ford even flew up from his California home to give the queen a personal tour of the Ford Presidential Museum in Grand Rapids. The queen and prince were my guests at a reception at the Amway Grand Plaza Hotel. The next day, there was a boat regatta on Lake Macatawa and Lake Michigan, and Queen Beatrix was quite pleased to find that we had arranged for her to be in the center of it all on board the Coast Guard cutter with Congressman and Mrs. Guy VanderJagt.

It also was a real treat for me to be able to bring my eighty-six-year-old father back to his home country to meet Queen Beatrix. He was keenly aware, I think, of the economic privations that forced his parents to emigrate to the United States in 1910 and was proud to return in triumph to the shore his father left. The Van Andel family had made a new start in America, but none of us ever forgot our Dutch heritage.

CHAPTER 11

The Responsibilities of Wealth

Since the late 1980s *Forbes* and other magazines have been including Rich and me on their vaunted billionaire lists. Neither Rich nor I have ever confirmed or denied such estimates—the magazines are free to speculate all they wish, but we will not give credence to their opinions by responding. Because Amway is a privately held company, we do not have to make available the same quantity of financial information that a publicly held company would. Often the magazine figures are off by a wide margin, and sometimes they're simply laughable. Guesses change drastically from year to year and even from month to month. In July of 1991, for instance, *Forbes* put Rich's and my wealth at $4.2 billion each. Three months later, *Forbes* revised their estimate downward to $3 billion each. In June of 1993, *Fortune* guessed that Rich and I were worth $3 billion each, but the October *Forbes* listed us as having $1.75 billion each. These wildly different estimates came during a time of strong, steady growth in Amway's sales. The publication of such lists does tend to put Rich and me in the limelight, which has its pluses (it provides some positive publicity for Amway) and minuses (we get some crazy letters). When I was first placed on the billionaire list, I received a seven- or eight-page letter from a European woman who spoke five languages, had a fabulous education, and had had at least two wealthy husbands. She told me all about herself and presented herself in the letter about as well as any corporate executive applying for a job. She made it very clear to me that she would like to meet me and said she could make my life "very enjoyable." I showed it to Bill Nicholson, who thought it was hilarious and made a copy to use in his college lectures on how to present oneself. It wasn't such a hit with Betty, of course, who was inclined to fly over to Europe and tell this high-priced courtesan to seek her prey elsewhere.

Coming into the public eye as a wealthy individual has some real dangers. Gerald Bremmer, a neighbor of mine at Lake Macatawa, wrote me early in 1979 to suggest it might be time to consider personal protection. For a long time, Rich and I both tried to ignore this fact, but by about 1980 we had gained such a high profile in the area that we had to take the step of hiring full-time security personnel. Several of these, Al Vander Wall, Rod Westveer, and Larry Mokma, have been with me and my family so much it sometimes seems that they're a part of the family.

Many Amway distributors I've spoken with want to know what it's like to be a billionaire. They want to hear, I suppose, about exotic sports cars, homes all over the world, weekends in Monaco, expensive jewelry, and private jets. All of those things are certainly nice to have, and I have enjoyed some of them. For me, however, the greatest pleasure comes not from the endless acquisition of material things but from creating wealth and giving it away. The task of every person on earth is to use everything he is given, every ability he has, to the ultimate glory of God. We are given physical and mental abilities and material wealth that we are expected to use to their highest and best potential. It does not matter how much or how little we are given—it only matters how we use what we do have. Jesus Christ taught of three servants who were each entrusted with large sums of money by their master. One received ten "talents," another five talents, and another one. After a long period of time, each was called to account. Two of the servants, who had invested the talents and doubled their master's money, were rewarded handsomely. The third, who had buried his talent and earned nothing for his master, was punished. The master took him to task for not even putting his money in the bank, where it could earn a market rate of return.

Just as in Jesus' parable, we are custodians of all the material wealth we are given. Each individual is required to use his wealth to do good. Sometimes that means giving away money; other times it means building something useful with it. Giving away one's wealth can benefit the individual, organization, or community that receives it immensely, but investing the wealth in a business can do something philanthropy cannot. Building a successful business creates wealth. Wealth creation benefits customers, employees, and business owners. Amway writes fourteen thousand paychecks every week, making fourteen thousand individuals and their families better off. Every item sold means that one customer is made better off. The entrepreneurs—the coordinators, planners, and risk takers—are made better off if they serve the customers well. Furthermore, each of these people is able to give away more money than they would have been able to otherwise. People who succeed create wealth and jobs and motivation and upward mobility for a great many people, not only for their family and friends but for many others as well.

When you achieve great wealth, priorities change. You can only wear one suit of clothing at a time; you can only drive one automobile at a time. Giving, however, is limitless. The first priority for Rich and me has been to keep the Amway business healthy and prosperous. We have an obligation to Amway customers, employees, and distributors. Beyond keeping the business healthy and profitable, however, we personally have an obligation to share our personal wealth. "He that hath a bountiful eye shall be blessed; for he giveth of his bread to the poor," wrote Solomon, the biblical philosopher-king.

The dispersal of personal wealth is not a choice. Wealth must be given away; there remains only one decision. Will it be given away during one's lifetime, or will it be distributed after one's death? Before death, the giver determines the amount and recipient of the wealth and is able to watch his wealth make a difference in the lives of the recipients. After death, in many cases, a large chunk of the wealth will go to the federal government, and the deceased misses out on the joy of giving.

THE MEANING OF GENEROSITY

When Alexis de Tocqueville came to America in 1831 to begin the work for his book *Democracy in America,* he was surprised at the philanthropic spirit of Americans. Everywhere he went in the United States he saw people having meetings. They were organizing into small charitable organizations at the community level, providing for their neighbors in need. Whether it was a health need, a tight financial time, a need for clothing for the children, or a place to live, some church or community organization would be there to assess those needs and give the necessary care. All of this occurred without government prompting or intervention because of a giving spirit in the hearts of Americans. Tocqueville was astounded—there was nothing like this in western Europe at the time.

Marvin Olasky, in his important book, *The Tragedy of American Compassion,* describes many of the thousands of nongovernmental charitable organizations that existed in nine-teenth-century America. These organizations, funded by the generosity of ordinary middle-class families, churches, and wealthy entrepreneurs, dealt compassionately and effectively with social problems similar to those we face today. Assistance was person-to-person, and generous enough to meet real needs, but administered so as not to engender unnecessary dependence on handouts. Moral accountability and training for productive jobs were central to these relief efforts.

Today the so-called compassionate liberals in the federal government have attempted to centralize charity. What this means, of course, is that what used to be effective church-based or community-based charity is now an involuntary income redistribution scheme administered from Washington. True charity has been replaced with a Robin Hood–like system of regular theft. Productive citizens who used to contribute to private charities now find their wealth diverted into poorly managed, ineffective government programs.

With government welfare programs there is little considera-tion of the real needs of the individual, almost no attempt to solve the root causes of poverty or ill health, and no real incen-tive for the people receiving government assistance to find per-manent solutions to their problems. The statists may pretend to have noble motives, but they are destroying a whole popula-tion with their "kindness."

Perhaps a worse consequence of welfare is that the basic human right of property is violated. Once our freedom to hold property (and dispose of it as we wish) is gone, other liberties are sure to be lost as well. Frédéric Bastiat, a nineteenth-century French economist, statesman, and author, believed in private charity but not the forced redistribution of wealth. In his best-known work, *The Law*, Bastiat writes,

> Whenever a portion of wealth is transferred from the person who owns it—without his consent and without compensation, and whether by force or by fraud—to anyone who does not own it, then I say that property is violated; that an act of plunder is committed.

I say that this act is exactly what the law is supposed to suppress, always and everywhere. When the law itself commits this act that it is supposed to suppress, I say that plunder is still committed, and I add that from the point of view of property and welfare, this aggression against rights is even worse.

Welfare programs in the United States today are a national embarrassment. In terms of their stated goals, they are a colossal failure. Americans have come to think of the poor as a permanent underclass, without hope of significant change. This pessimistic view of individual initiative suggests that the best we can do is provide lower-income people with a check every month to take care of their basic needs. Sometimes that is the *worst* thing to do for people in need. When pushed by necessity, people draw on their inner strengths and special abilities to climb to levels of achievement they never thought possible. Most people have the ability and the wherewithal to perform these feats of entrepreneurship, but often it takes economic hardship to bring it out of them. In fact, just handing out money to people in need is the surest way to keep them there.

Government is notoriously one of the worst ways of accomplishing almost any sort of business in this country. And certainly, handing over the business of charity to government has not been a very successful venture for us.

Rich and I, and several other businessmen in the Grand Rapids area, have tried to promote economic development through our area's Right Place Program instead of expanded welfare programs. We haven't forgotten the importance of charitable giving, of course, but we try to keep it community-based. By directing our giving toward local organizations, such as our local church, we're just acting in accordance with commonly accepted views on how to be generous for maximum effect. We believe that our approach can reduce poverty much more effectively than current government programs.

Boosting the local economy raises the standard of living for nearly everyone in the area, so that the poverty that inspires welfare programs is reduced. With that in mind, Rich and I and Amway have contributed heavily to the revitalization of downtown Grand Rapids. Each project we conducted has been evaluated for community impact and consistency with our Christian principles. Our efforts might be called the "free-enterprise approach to urban renewal." Though some projects have made use of available municipal, state, and federal funds, private investments have been the driving force behind the Grand Rapids downtown revival. The projects we've helped fund have generally been well placed, well timed, and well organized, we believe.

HOME IMPROVEMENT

One of the biggest and best ways that Rich and I were able to improve the Grand Rapids area was to refurbish and expand a large hotel in the middle of downtown. In 1978 Amway was the largest user of hospitality facilities in western Michigan, with our annual convention alone bringing in some ten thousand people, and hundreds more every week. The facilities in the area were not adequate for us and had not been for years. The brand-new convention center downtown provided the kernel for future growth. Rich and our friend, Dick Gillett, had spearheaded the fund-raising for the convention center and thus provided the spark plug for future development, but the center could not function at its best without a major new hotel. Various people had proposed hotels in recent years, but the plans generally evaporated. So I sat down one day with Rich and said, "Well, it seems to me that if we're going to be able to utilize that convention center that we helped to bring about, we're going to have to have a hotel." He agreed, so we sent a proposal to Walt Sowles, the city's development coordinator, and his committee was happy to see what we could do with our plans.

In August of 1978, then, we bought the Pantlind Hotel on Pearl Street, with an idea of renovating the historic hotel and building a high-rise with additional rooms in the immediate area. The Pantlind purchase was a combination business decision and heart decision. The Pantlind was *the* hotel in Grand Rapids from its opening in 1916 up through the forties and fifties. When I was growing up in the area, the Pantlind was the symbol of something almost unachievable, something so magnificent that one could only dream of staying a night in the place. It was quite a treat to even eat out at the Pantlind. People didn't dine out as much as they do today—perhaps only once or twice a year. The Pantlind delivered excellent cuisine and impeccable service, cultivating a reputation as one of the Midwest's finest hotels. In the Pantlind's prime, Grand Rapids was enjoying an age of elegance made available by the thriving furniture industry and a migration west from the big eastern cities. We were eager to bring a world-class hotel back to town.

The project was completed in two phases. First, we began renovating the Pantlind. When it reopened in 1981 as the Amway Grand Plaza Hotel, the renewed edifice was indisputably a world-class hotel. It offered 395 deluxe rooms, six restaurants and lounges, and several fine retail shops. In addition, there was convenient access to a new downtown convention center and DeVos Hall, a two-thousand-seat concert hall to which Rich and Helen were major contributors. Lush in historical decor, with traditional, luxurious furnishings (made in Grand Rapids), the rooms recalled the grandeur of the 1900s. A professional staff with world-class chefs and a European-style concierge helped make a stay at the Amway Grand Plaza Hotel at least as memorable as a stay at the Pantlind used to be. The dedication of the new hotel on September 15 coincided with the opening of the new Grand Rapids Art Museum on the 17th and the Gerald Ford Presidential Museum on the 18th. The whole city of Grand Rapids turned out to have a party in their rejuvenated downtown in six days of festivities called the "Celebration on the Grand." There were fireworks, sports events, a hot-air balloon race, and merchants' festivals. *Good Morning, America* broadcast from Grand Rapids, and Larry King and Bob Hope hosted special shows. Ronald Reagan, Gerald Ford, and Canadian prime minister Pierre Trudeau all made appearances, and former French president Valéry Giscard d'Estaing and former secretaries of state Henry Kissinger and Alexander Haig were also present.

So many political leaders were there in Grand Rapids that it only made sense for some of them to take the opportunity to meet together. On September 17, then, President Reagan met with Trudeau and President José Lopez Portillo of Mexico. Al Haig, who was present for that first meeting, told me later that it was "tense." Reagan and Trudeau were not exactly seeing eye to eye on a number of important issues, and there were some issues with Mexico to be cleared up. There were some disputes with the Canadians over West Coast and New England fisheries as well as an Alaska-to-Northeast U.S. gas pipeline that led to quite heated discussions with Trudeau. On the Mexican side, drug smuggling and illegal immigration along the rather porous border were creating tensions. The next morning, the group met again in the Lumber Barons Bar (now Tinseltown) of the Amway Grand Plaza Hotel for a continental breakfast and further discussion. It was a momentous occasion for all three nations, and a bronze plaque now marks the site of their meeting in the hotel.

The second phase of the hotel project was the construction of a twenty-nine-story glass-sheathed tower between the former Pantlind and the riverfront. The tower project was even more exciting for me than the restoration of the Pantlind. Paired with the historic edifice, the 316-foot structure would reflect Grand Rapids' "Age of Elegance" as well as the urban revival that the city was experiencing. The early blueprints showed an aggressive yet simple structure that would redefine the skyline of Grand Rapids. Initially, the building was conceived to be built not on the riverbank but astride the Grand River itself, with the river flowing underneath. But then there was the problem of who owned the river and who owned the river bottom, so we decided to plant the building on solid ground. The tower would add nearly three hundred deluxe rooms and suites, more retail space, and one of the finest restaurants in Grand Rapids, the Cygnus. Today, six other restaurants and four lounges offer everything from deli-style sandwiches and pizza to gourmet cuisine. When the weather is bad, guests can shop in the retail stores located in the hotel or walk to other downtown attractions through the network of skywalks.

One year to the day after the dedication of the renewed Pantlind, Rich and I "lit up the town" with a "topping-off" ceremony for the new tower. A crowd of about 1,500 gathered on the opposite bank of the river in front of the Gerald R. Ford Presidential Museum to participate. Under umbrellas in a steady drizzling rain, I struggled to make a speech with water sluicing onto the script I was trying to follow. Rich was no help at all. "I hate to say this, Jay," he said, "but I think you're all wet." After our hurried speeches there was a brief twenty-nine-story light show on the river side of the new tower, with 1,400 colored lights and stellar accompaniment from the Grand Rapids Symphonic Band.

The topping-off ceremony was the opening event for another "Celebration on the Grand," and there was plenty to celebrate. The $60 million Amway Grand Plaza Hotel project was just one of a half-dozen downtown projects that promised to bring people back into the central city. The conventions that the hotel–civic center combination could bring in, however, were the key to bringing merchants back downtown. When the merchants moved downtown to capture business from the conventions, Grand Rapids natives would follow the merchants. A positive development cycle would begin that could boost growth for decades, and the new Van Andel Arena has accelerated that development.

BUILDING A DREAM

We were pleased to see that the new hotel complex soon received the AAA Four Star rating for the quality and value of our accommodations. The hotel has been extremely successful, has maintained a high quality rating for many years, and has proven itself to be one of the cornerstones of the rebuilding of downtown Grand Rapids. In fact, it was so much fun that we've since tackled several other downtown projects that have revitalized our city.

One of these was a new museum. In 1989, after much political rhetoric about a new museum, a fund-raising drive formally began. Dubbing the campaign "It's About Time," Grand Rapids citizens sought to gather over $30 million in funds for construction over a three-year period. I was asked to chair the fund-raising committee. With Casey Wondergem's assistance, we managed to raise a large portion of the funds for the museum from thousands of corporate and individual donors in the Grand Rapids area. Betty and I personally contributed $7.4 million toward the project. Recognition was not limited to the large donors—anyone could help out simply by purchasing a brick inscribed with their name, to be placed in a special wall in the museum. Today, across the Grand River from the Amway Grand Plaza Hotel sits the new "Van Andel Museum Center and Roger B. Chaffee Planetarium." The next major project we took on was the funding of a sports and entertainment arena in downtown Grand Rapids. Rich and I had long felt that an arena would be a valuable addition to the downtown area and to the community, and city leaders had expressed a desire to bring events to town that existing facilities couldn't handle.

Rich's son Dick had the foresight early on to organize a group called "Grand Vision," which represented various segments of the public and private sector interested in sports and entertainment. The group's purpose was to achieve consensus on the need and location for a new arena. As Dick said later, "There seemed to be a real sense of desire in the community, but all the right factors weren't together. I asked that initial group of community leaders and activists, 'Does this make sense or doesn't it? If it does, then let's get on with it. If it doesn't, then let's get it off the agenda.'" Early on, when Dick's group needed to come up with a preliminary design for the building, to see if the project was financially feasible, I donated the funds necessary to draw up and evaluate the project. A consensus began to congeal around the idea, and Dick's group changed from Grand Vision to Grand Action (which Dick still cochairs with John Canepa and David Frey as we move from the arena to the proposed new convention center).

Dick made a lot of good arguments in favor of the arena. An arena gives people more options for entertainment, so instead

of sitting in front of a TV, people go to the Grand Rapids downtown to have a good time. By drawing people from out of town
to the downtown area, an arena also boosts the hotel and
restaurant business. In combination with all the other attractions in downtown Grand Rapids, the arena contributes to the
revitalization and growth of the central city. The economic
impact study Dick's group conducted showed that the arena
would generate extremely positive effects for the entire city.

Our fund-raising efforts were very successful with the arena
as they were with the museum. The city got behind the project
and proved that the arena would be well used and appreciated.
Originally, my gift was to be $8 million, but as costs mounted,
Betty and I ended up providing $11.5 million for what is now
the Van Andel Arena. Architecturally, the arena is a masterpiece
of design and creativity. The impressive glass-sheathed exterior
stands apart in the historic Grand Rapids downtown, but it
takes nothing away from the atmosphere. It is forward looking,
but not pushy with its presence; it is dynamic, but not overly
aggressive. Skywalks connect the arena to the 682-room, four-
star Amway Grand Plaza Hotel, The Courtyard by Marriott,
the Plaza Towers, and other major downtown buildings.

The arena provided a wonderful opportunity to introduce a
new professional sports team to the community. My son Dave
and Rich's son Dan, along with other city leaders, led the campaign to bring a professional ice hockey team to the Grand
Rapids area. Since its opening in October 1996, the twelve-
thousand-seat arena has been the home of the Grand Rapids
Griffins, of the International Hockey League. The first few
months of operation indicated that the arena would be a great
success. It drew more visitors than expected and gave a big
boost to the downtown economy. From the October opening
to the end of 1997, 451,000 people attended arena events—11
percent more than anticipated.

PLAZA TOWERS

Most recently, Amway undertook a massive renovation of a *new* building in downtown Grand Rapids. That's right, new. In 1992 a just-completed hotel/condominium/apartment building began having some serious problems. The $39 million Eastbank Waterfront Towers complex had been built on a tight budget by an out-of-town developer, and it showed. The exterior brick panels leaked, bathroom exhaust was being blown back into the building, and the iron piping for the air-conditioning was rapidly corroding—in a building just a few months old!

Originally, Amway was to manage the hotel part of the building, but when we saw that the building was such a lemon, we backed out. But with the project heading toward bankruptcy, we decided our history of involvement in the downtown area required us to turn a lemon into lemonade. Initially we had to decide whether to just tear the building down or completely renovate it. Rich and I like to think of ourselves as builders, not destroyers, so we spent another $40 million to completely overhaul the interior and exterior. Completed in June of 1997, The Plaza Towers, as it is now called, is a fully occupied structure gracing the skyline of our city. In addition to the residences, the tower also has a Courtyard by Marriott hotel, offices, a gift shop, and a health club.

Naturally, I'm thrilled to be a part of such a successful series of projects that have added so much to my hometown and its people. But in a sense, I had to do it. If I truly believe all that I have preached about free enterprise and business, I couldn't stand by and let the government do it. All of these projects prove that what works best is when the private sector partners with government to turn a city into a beautiful, functional place to live, work, and play.

In fact, without the benefit of private participation, govern-ment planning and funding of projects can make a good idea a failure, or a make a bad idea much worse. Look at the down-town areas of many cities in the United States and the evidence is plainly seen. Slums created by rent control, building restrictions, and other foolish government policies scar the inner city. Downtown businesses hover inches from bankruptcy, suffering from insufficient parking, poor crime control, and government subsidization of suburban competitors. Then city planners, acting without the benefit of private-sector input, decide to "solve" the problem that government created by building a horrendously expensive, taxpayer-funded stadium or some other boondoggle that leaves the community with foolish amounts of debt.

A more sensible solution is to allow private corporations and individuals to search out the needs of the community and fill those needs appropriately. Government planners, blinded to the real needs of the community by political motives and incapacitated by poor information, are not nearly as good at serving people as private firms and community-minded individuals.

CHAPTER 12

Entering
Politics

I got involved in politics the way a lot of people do. I saw how the political process could affect my life, so I began taking an active interest in what our elected officials were doing. For me, that meant serving on the Ada Planning Commission in the 1960s. The commission was in charge of zoning property in the area, which was supposed to increase the tax base and provide Ada citizens with employment closer to home. As the fastest growing business in the area, Rich and I wanted to make sure that Amway was represented.

From the local level my activity expanded to the state level when, in 1971, Governor George Romney appointed me to the Michigan State Compensation Commission. This is a commis-

sion set up to set the salaries of elected officials. My chairmanship there gave me a window into the political scene and
allowed me to make some contacts in state government. It was
difficult work, the job paid no salary, and it made some legislators very angry with me because I refused to pay them what
they thought they were worth. I stuck it out, however, and was
reappointed by Governor Bill Milliken, who succeeded
Governor Romney. As I saw more of what political life was
like, I moved into more active involvement with the
Republican Party in an effort to change things for the better.

Governor Milliken came over to see me one day in 1973
and asked me to become the chairman of the Republican State
Finance Committee. Though the party was totally broke at the
time, I accepted, and Bill and I together accomplished a lot for
the Republican Party. He would throw fund-raising parties in
Lansing, and our committee was asked to help fill the place
with Republican Party supporters. The first time I spoke in
Lansing, I pointed out the importance of having a financially
stable party. "The first priority is this debt," I said. "It's got to
go. And we're going to stay out of debt. How can the
Republican Party have any credibility with people when our
state finances are a mess?" Thanks to many generous supporters, we were able to take the party from minus a million dollars in the treasury to plus a million dollars in the treasury in a
year's time.

I supported a large number of Republican legislators
through my donations to the party, beginning with those close
to home, in Michigan, and later those on the national scene. I
strongly believe that political parties should be the soliciting
and disbursing agencies for political contributions, not candidates or candidate committees. For this reason, the bulk of my
political contributions were made to the Republican Party, not
to individual candidates. Whenever I did donate to specific
candidates, I always tried to support those who I learned were

honest and moral. This country desperately needs more responsible, moral politicians. Some might think that's an oxy-moron, but there are many legislators whom I know personally who are morally upright and sound on the issues as well, including our own congressman, Vern Ehlers, who replaced the late Paul Henry.

The late Paul Henry was one of those men I considered to be an ideal legislator. He was an honest man, someone who represented his constituents well. Paul was a philosopher, too; a onetime professor at Calvin College, he was a scholar rather than a mere legal technician. The philosophers speculate about the "ought"; most politicians these days seem to concentrate on the "is." I think Congress would be much stronger today if we could replace some of the all-too-pragmatic lawyers with some solid-thinking philosophers. It was a rare pleasure of mine to enjoy a deep philosophical and theological conversation with Paul. That ability must have come from his father, Carl Henry, who is probably one of the finest Protestant theologians in the country.

My introduction to national politics came through my work with the U.S. Chamber of Commerce. The mission of the Chamber of Commerce was attractive to me because of its emphasis on industry, not government, as a source of economic growth. I began working with the chamber at the state level in the 1960s and was eventually elected chairman of the board of the Michigan State Chamber of Commerce in 1970. This gained me the attention of people in the national organization, and in 1972 I was elected to the national board of directors.

After seven years on the national board, I was elected to a term as chairman of the board. That was a very exciting, ful-filling time for me. The chairmanship provided me with an opportunity to speak in defense of free enterprise all over the United States, and I took full advantage of that. After my chairmanship was up, I continued to be active in the chamber by serving as chairman of the Executive Committee. The chamber had a term limit on its board of directors (a policy I wish the U.S. Congress would adopt!), so in 1985, after fourteen years on the board, I completed my term and turned my attention elsewhere.

FLIGHT TO FREEDOM

One of the most interesting political organizations with which I was involved was the Jamestown Foundation, which I helped found in 1983. The cold war was in high gear at that time, and the State Department was not doing a good job of making the best of opportunities to use defectors in consulting and other such positions. Former KGB agents, high-ranking members of the Soviet military, and other high-level Soviet defectors found themselves working in low-paying, menial jobs after the U.S. government had debriefed them. This concerned those of us who believed that these people could contribute a great deal more to this country. The Jamestown Foundation was formed to help these people adjust to life in America and place them where they would be respected and used to greater advantage.

The Jamestown Foundation gave me a window into life behind the Iron Curtain. At a 1989 Jamestown Foundation benefit dinner in Washington, D.C., it was my privilege to meet a group of prominent Soviet defectors, including former KGB agents, former diplomats, and high-ranking Soviet army officers. At my table were Secretary of Defense Dick Cheney and defector Arkady Shevchenko. Shevchenko's 1978 defection was big news in the United States, as he was a former undersecretary general of the United Nations and had been a close personal advisor to Andrei Gromyko. His intriguing book *Breaking with Moscow,* which he wrote after his defection, became a best-seller in the United States. In the remarks I gave at that dinner, I spoke of the great personal sacrifices these defectors had made and the reminders they provided us of the value of freedom. Some of these brave people had tasted life outside the Soviet Union, while others had only heard about it by rumor. In spite of the risks and obvious cost in personal pain, they believed it was worth giving up their homeland in order to gain basic human liberties.

Now that the Iron Curtain has collapsed, the Jamestown Foundation is working to get the word out on what's happening inside formerly communist nations—providing up-to-date information on their growth and development and giving us details on what we might be concerned about as Americans. I'm no longer personally involved with the work of the Jamestown Foundation, but I'm proud to see that what I helped begin is continuing to produce fruit.

I was also privileged to serve on the board of the National Endowment for Democracy from its beginnings in 1983. The congressionally funded NED is a bipartisan group whose mission is to give financial and technical support to groups working for democracy throughout the world. With a relatively tiny budget and unobtrusive methods, the NED manages to give these groups decisive influence. In 1988, funds from the NED helped two hundred thousand poor Chileans obtain the small photographs required of voters, which contributed to a huge voter turnout and a narrow victory over the Pinochet dictatorship. We would also provide copiers, printing presses, and other equipment and materials to support groups struggling to change oppressive regimes. It's difficult to know what effect this had, but I envisioned members of a small, struggling opposition group making thousands of fliers on a NED copier, then handing them out on the streets at great risk to themselves. I am convinced that the NED's work had a lot to do with the collapse of communism worldwide in the early 1990s.

My introduction to the NED actually came about through my work for the U.S. Chamber of Commerce. The chamber was to be one of four "core" groups behind the NED, and I fell into a role as the chamber's representative on the board of directors. The first organizational meeting of the NED brought together some prominent business and union leaders, including Lane Kirkland, the head of the American Federation of Labor. These people were all sitting around trying to decide whom to elect as treasurer, when Lane said, "Well, it's got to be Jay Van Andel—he's got so much money that he'd never bother to steal our money. Let's elect him!" So that settled it, and I served for a while as the NED treasurer.

As much as my political philosophy differed from the philosophies of some of the other individuals sitting around the boardroom table at the NED, I was greatly impressed by the unity we all had in the basic idea of a democratic form of government. When we considered the violence and tyranny that characterized many nondemocratic governments around the world, our political differences in the United States seemed much less important.

A PLACE FOR POLITICS

Why did I feel it necessary to be so politically active? Many advocates of big government wished I were less so. But for me it was a responsibility that I had—a duty to be involved in the civil arena. The tenuous nature of this country's very survival called me to run onto the political battlefield. For me, it was a religious call as well. Some say that religion and politics don't mix, or that politics is "dirty" and Christians shouldn't be involved. It was apparent to me that religion was already in politics—the religion of statism. When the citizens of a country call on the almighty state for food and housing and clothing, for protection from natural disasters, for education—in short, for all their worldly needs—then the state is a god to those people.

My Dutch Calvinist background also provided much of the impetus behind my activity. The French theologian and one-time governor of Geneva, John Calvin, believed that because man is basically prone to do evil, there must be a civil magistrate to restrain him. Many politicians have no problem with this idea. I know this because they take this to an extreme, sending out armies of bureaucrats to restrain people from doing what they believe is evil. But they often miss the second part of Calvin's teaching on the state. The civil magistrate, Calvin taught, was also prone to do evil, and for this reason he needed to be restrained as well. Thus, in John Calvin we find the religious basis for constitutionally limited government.

In 1900 Holland had a prime minister who fervently believed, with most of his countrymen of the time, that Christian principles applied to politics as well as any other part of life. His name was Abraham Kuyper. Kuyper heartily believed in the separation of church and state, but he maintained that the civil government had a responsibility before God to perform definite tasks. Because of man's propensity toward evil, the government was necessary "to thwart all license and outrage and to shield the good against the evil." "The highest duty of the government," Kuyper wrote, "remains . . . unchangeably that of justice. . . ." The government was also morally required to stay out of certain areas of people's lives: "In a Calvinistic sense . . . the family, the business, science, art and so forth are all social spheres, which do not owe their existence to the state, and which do not derive the law of their life from the superiority of the state. . . ." Abraham Kuyper neatly dismisses the notion that the state has unlimited jurisdiction, calling instead for protection of each sphere of authority against interference by the others. While civil government is clearly necessary under Kuyper's sphere sovereignty, certain "spheres" of human activity are off-limits to state intervention. Thus, as Kuyper put it, "the State may never become an octopus, which stifles the whole of life. It must occupy its own place, on its own root, among all the other trees of the forest, and thus it has to honor and maintain every form of life which grows independently in its own sacred autonomy."

Without a clear understanding of the principles Kuyper taught, we are likely to fall into serious errors. President Clinton, quite rightly, asked recently that every church in America provide one job to someone on welfare. It shouldn't take a presidential reminder to motivate the church; this is exactly the kind of individual-oriented provision for the poor to which God has called Christians. But some in the church have protested against this call to ecclesiastical responsibility. One Reverend Albert Pennybacker, of the National Council of Churches, responded to Clinton in the March 17, 1997, issue of *Time* magazine by saying, "Our job is not to compensate for the failure of the government to do its job."

Reverend Pennybacker's comment reveals his lack of understanding of Kuyper's sphere sovereignty principle. Job provision does not lie within the sphere of civil government but is the domain of individual entrepreneurs. When government tries to intervene, it usually results in fewer jobs and less productivity in the long run. Rather than take over the task of job provision, government should get out of the way of private business and private charity. Entrepreneurs create productive jobs and discover other ways to satisfy human needs, and charitable institutions help those who cannot provide adequately for their own needs.

Individuals, families, churches, and civil governments, then, all have their own realms. The individual and each institution he is involved in are important to the prosperity of a nation. Civil government is not the only, or even the highest, of human institutions. Before the federal government dramatically expanded its domain in the 1930s, this was more clearly understood in the United States. Families, churches, and neighborly relationships stabilized and governed society—civil government was unneeded and unwanted in many situations. These other institutions were highly effective in educating children, promoting decency and civility, providing for the needs of the poor, and even keeping crime to a minimum. Churches were a source of spiritual nourishment and material care, as congregations cared for the needs of those within their membership and those in the community at large. Locally run mutual aid societies, friends, families, and neighbors assisted in taking care of the poor and the disabled.

The family and the church play important roles in the life of a society because they are durable institutions. Families maintain continuity from one generation to the next—encouraging socially acceptable behavior, providing emotional, physical, and material support, and teaching language, culture, and morals. Without the training, support, discipline, and love of families, civilization as we know it would fall apart. Churches, in addition to their function as centers of worship, preserve across thousands of years those moral traditions that are essential for the rule of law. Without the rule of law, society would quickly deteriorate into an anarchic mess in which industry and commerce would be impossible. Moral teaching about promise-keeping and respecting the belongings of others discourages people from breaking contracts and permits businesses to function for the benefit of the whole economy.

To prevent the civil government from usurping the roles of these other institutions, thereby destroying their effectiveness, the civil government must be limited by traditional moral principles. Each institution in society is necessarily limited in its power by the other institutions, and ultimately by the people. This applies no less to the state. Because we're all human and subject to human failings, the ruler's urge to have unlimited power should be strictly restrained by the people. Every citizen must be vigilant, because every king, every president, every prime minister, every senator, every city councilman, and every sheriff is tempted to abuse authority. Today it seems that assuming responsibility for one's own life is a rarer and rarer thing. It's easier, in a limited sense, to abdicate responsibility, to ask the government to do what we all ought to be doing on our own and with the help of our families, churches, and other organizations in the private sector. What people seem to forget is that someone has to pay for all of that, and always, that someone is us, through taxes. And as you might guess, I don't think higher and higher taxes help business or individuals.

CHAPTER 13

Who Spends Your Money Best?

The tax-and-spend fiscal policy that has character-ized nearly every Democratic administration in modern history is one of the most destructive political and economic forces ever to plague this nation. The most notorious example of this came during President Jimmy Carter's administration. At the time, I was serving with the U.S. Chamber of Commerce, where we felt the best thing government could do to help the economy was to reduce taxes and spending. But according to President Carter and the spendthrifts in Congress, spending was the key to economic growth. So if the American people didn't spend enough on their own, by golly, they didn't know what was good for them. The all-wise government should tax their money away from them and spend it.

What the Carter administration and Congress didn't understand was that it wasn't spending but investment that drives the economy. Investment, in the long run, will make everyone better off by increasing the productive capacity of the economy. This was misunderstood by Carter and by most other Democratic presidents of our century. The interest rates of up to 21 percent that resulted from Carter's misguided economics discouraged investment and dragged down the whole economy. As a consequence, real income for the average American family fell from 1977 to 1981. Only the income of the wealthiest 1 percent of Americans grew during the Carter years. That's why I am always baffled when liberals chant their mantra that cutting taxes only benefits the rich. Here was a clear example of how increased taxes hurt the average taxpayer while the wealthy benefited.

When President Reagan's generous investment tax credit and other tax changes came about in 1981, some people supposed it to be another way for rich capital owners to stick it to labor. A moment's thought reveals this to be untrue. Who accomplishes more—a man with a shovel or a man with a bulldozer? Clearly the man with the heavy equipment is able to do more, and he will enjoy part of the additional profits that his increased productivity generates. The capital investor—the person who invested in the heavy equipment—increased the productivity of labor and consequently increased the return to labor. What happened to the well-being of the average American? It increased. Reversing the trend from the Carter years, average real family income grew by well over 15 percent from 1982 to 1989. This growth included all income groups from the poorest to the richest. And the growth was consistent. From 1982 through 1990, Americans enjoyed a new peacetime record of ninety-six continuous months of economic growth.

BELT-TIGHTENING

Tax-and-spend policies are all the more dangerous because they are difficult to reverse. Government taxes and spends for two basic reasons. First, tax-and-spend policies are aimed at meeting macroeconomic goals such as lower unemployment and higher real income. They may meet these goals in the short run, but in the long run tax-and-spend policies will result in higher unemployment and lower real income. Second, government budgets are used to garner votes for the politicians writing the budgets. Dishonest politicians stop writing laws that benefit everyone and write laws that take wealth from everyone in order to benefit special-interest groups. The state becomes, as the French economist Frédéric Bastiat put it, "that great fictitious entity by which everyone seeks to live at the expense of everyone else." This is precisely why it is so difficult to cut spending: Every American has one or more favorite government programs that he doesn't want to see cut. Any politician who suggests that a government spending program be cut will be immediately bombarded by complaints and threats from one or more special-interest groups. The legislator's mailbox will be crammed with letters condemning him for promoting "job losses" and for opposing "the common good." Never mind that budget cutting increases job opportunities and enhances the well-being of everyone in the long run. If we could all give up our favorite programs, the whole of American society would benefit immeasurably.

There are about 1,400 federal benefit programs in effect today. To reduce government spending and the size of government, people are going to have to give up some of these programs. Where necessary, the private sector will step in to provide for human needs where the government steps out. Because private charities and other organizations can work more efficiently and with more focus on the individual, they will do a better job of filling those needs than the government ever did.

What is needed is a bit of short-run belt-tightening. The businessman who is receiving a government-guaranteed loan will have to forgo it. The farmer who is receiving a price support will have to give it up. The mother who is having her child's school lunch paid for by the taxpayers will have to pay for it herself or get a charity to help her. The professor who is receiving a grant to study the sex life of a Brazilian frog will have to persuade some research group, corporation, or private individual to give him that grant. The artist who is receiving government funds to produce bad art that nobody wants to buy will have to go out in the open market and produce pictures that somebody wants. The food-stamp recipient will have to apply to a local church or charitable organization for help. The college student who's getting a government grant to go to college will have to apply for a scholarship or go out and work for the tuition instead. The politician who lives by taking money out of everyone's pockets and handing it to those who curry favor with him is going to have to get an honest job.

The truth is that government redistribution has invaded almost every facet of our society, and, therefore, a cutback in the size of government is going to affect almost everybody. And unless we, as a nation, collectively and individually are willing to accept the temporary costs of that cutback, we cannot enjoy the sizable long-run benefits.

Cutbacks in spending will result in a higher growth rate and lower interest rates. Higher growth rates aren't just numbers that make economists happy. Higher growth rates mean a higher standard of living for ourselves, for our children, and for our grandchildren. Whatever short-term sacrifices we make, they will be more than made up for by dramatic increases in wealth in the not-too-distant future.

The key to a higher rate of growth is simply for the government to allow the private sector to do what it does best. The private sector is able and willing to take over from federal and state governments in providing scholarships, charitable gifts, grants, loans, and other support. And the private sector can do all of this in a business-healthy, economy-healthy way that benefits all of us.

A BETTER TAX SYSTEM

One way to reduce the damage that tax-and-spend politicians produce would be to create a less destructive tax system. If we had deliberately set out to invent the most complicated, unfair, argumentative, expensive, and inefficient way to collect federal taxes, we would probably have come up with a system closely resembling what we have today. In three separate studies with which I was closely involved, undertaken by the U.S. Chamber of Commerce, Citizen's Choice, and the Heritage Foundation, it was found that the American individual and corporate income taxes were among the most senseless ways to collect federal revenues that could possibly be devised.

The modern income tax, introduced with the Sixteenth Amendment in 1913, has far-reaching, devastating effects on our economy. Number two on Marx and Engels's list of ten objectives in *The Communist Manifesto,* the progressive income tax allows for income redistribution on a grand scale. Once this immoral process has started, there is no clear end to it. If it is good to take a little from one by force and give to another, then perhaps it is better to take more from one by force and give to another, or to expand the number of recipients. The final end is that instead of simply helping the poor, the unemployed, and the handicapped, a vast army of others with questionable needs gets in line for the handouts also. Ultimately, so many are on the receiving end that it becomes politically impossible to control. What started as a moral problem rapidly becomes a political and economic problem. We take so much from the productive to pay the nonproductive that we create a new class of Americans who live off other people's taxes. All the while the "compassionate" statist is pretending that this institutionalized pork barrel is only for the sake of the poor. The productive slow down, and the pie inevitably gets smaller for everyone. In the end, as Warren Brookes puts it, "The attempt to redistribute wealth by redistributing money through the progressive tax tables only winds up keeping the poor poor, the rich rich, and the middle class struggling even harder to keep up with taxation."

Exacerbating the problems of the progressive income tax are the difficulties of understanding the tax code. It's bad enough when it takes a whole day (or more) out of an ordinary citizen's year to file taxes, or when that citizen gives up and pays a large fee to a tax preparer. Things are made worse when even the IRS tax advisors can't be relied upon for accurate help.

The tax issue was important to Amway and to me personally. Due to the complexity of the tax code and some personal misunderstandings of what Amway was all about, some distributors had run into problems with the IRS. In 1982, Congress and the IRS investigated some large deductions being taken by some Amway distributors. Some people, it seemed, had started Amway businesses not as a legitimate moneymaking enterprise but as a tax shelter. Some stretching of IRS rules concerning business expense deductions had occurred, and several distributors found themselves facing the not-so-friendly side of the IRS. Distributors who get carried away looking for tax-reducing gimmicks are confused as to the purpose of Amway, so we cooperated with the IRS to communicate the problem to our distributors and put a stop to the tax evasion.

Part of the problem stemmed from an ex-IRS revenue agent turned Amway distributor. This self-proclaimed expert in taxes provided other distributors with a cleverly done but distorted and unreasonable interpretation of the tax law. Some of the distributors who heard him entered into some creative but misguided strategies to enhance their deductions and hurt not only themselves but the entire Amway organization.

With a no-frills flat tax, there are no deductions to confuse taxpayers and enrich tax lawyers, no ambiguous rules to be stretched. The IRS can release most of its enforcement staff to more productive employment, because there is not as much room to cheat. While I was chairman of the national Chamber of Commerce I spoke out in favor of a low flat-rate tax with no deductions whatsoever. Several years later, in the summer of 1985, I testified before a House Ways and Means subcommittee in support of Reagan's proposed reform of the federal income tax system. The federal tax system had spiraled out of control, and Reagan's proposal was the beginning of a return to tax sanity. As I testified, almost three million Americans were working full-time on federal tax compliance activities. The private-sector tax compliance workforce was almost thirty-two times the ninety-three-thousand-person workforce of the IRS. Even though the tax law Reagan proposed retained deductions and a progressive rate structure, I supported it because it was a vast improvement over the previous system. My ideal was still a deduction-free flat tax, but a true flat-tax bill would never have passed the Ninety-ninth Congress.

Tax laws, I told the subcommittee, should not be used to effect social or economic policy. A tax law should be used solely to collect revenues as fairly, simply, and efficiently as possible. I argued further that corporate profits should not be used as a tax base at all. First of all, "corporate profits" are difficult to define and bring onto the scene an unnecessary army of lawyers, tax accountants, and IRS auditors. Reagan's proposal didn't eliminate that problem, but it did move things in the right direction, I think. Second, any corporate tax is passed on to individuals in some form. Customers pay higher prices, workers receive lower wages, and stockholders face lower returns. So the corporate profit tax is essentially a deceptive, hidden tax to the individual. At the same time, the corporation's competitors may pay little or no taxes, which warps and stifles the equity of our basic free-enterprise system.

Profit taxes tax only the competent and successful; the big spenders who keep little profit, the sloppy operators, the incompetent, are allowed to go tax free. Fast-growing, high-profit businesses that might one day compete successfully with the Japanese or the European Community find their growth stunted by these taxes. Small businesses, needing capital to grow but unable to issue stock, are denied a large part of an important source of funds for expansion. To tax these profits is to stifle business.

Reagan's tax reform proposal was supposed to be "revenue neutral," which meant that the total taxes taken from the private sector would stay the same. Changing the tax code around did nothing to ease the total tax burden on the American people, but it did make the burden a little more equitable, and it made the tax code a little less complex.

Reagan's 1981 Economic Recovery Tax Act, which took full effect in 1984, reduced marginal tax rates across the board. In 1986 the Tax Reform Act cut the top rate nearly in half, from 50 percent to 28 percent. Was this unfair to lower-income Americans? No. Because of the vast increase in productivity that resulted from the tax cuts, the revenue share from high-income Americans increased even though the marginal tax rates had dropped. In 1980, Americans in the top 1 percent of gross income were paying 19.3 percent of total federal individual income taxes. By 1988, at the end of the Reagan era, that income group was paying 27.6 percent. Reagan's flatter tax rate structure resulted in a shift of the individual income tax burden away from lower- and middle-income Americans onto higher-income Americans.

The next step would be a flat tax along the lines of what Steve Forbes suggested in his 1996 bid for the Republican nomination for president. A flat tax would be simpler, fairer, and less expensive to implement. A tax return could fit on a postcard that would take about three minutes to fill out. My federal tax return has 1,200 pages. Most Americans don't have quite that many forms to fill out, but it can nevertheless take a lot of time to satisfy the IRS with the proper paperwork. And I mean a lot of time. Americans devote about 5.4 billion hours a year to federal tax-related paperwork. If we consider that people could be working at a productive job during this time, this daunting task becomes an annual drain of $159 billion out of the economy, according to *Costly Returns,* a 1993 book by James Payne. Droves of tax accountants and tax lawyers, not to mention the enormous bureaucracy that is the IRS, are required to support the income tax system. Imagine how much better off our economy could be if these well-trained, highly intelligent people were turned loose from tax calculation to work at more productive jobs!

Legislators should consider the opinion of my friend Ed Feulner. Mincing no words, Ed proposes "that Washington leave the doggone tax code alone—declare a moratorium on tax bills—until it is ready to do what really needs to be done. That is: Chuck the entire seventeen-thousand-plus-page tax code into Washington's biggest trash can and replace it with a simple, flat tax that everyone can understand without the help of an accountant, lawyer, or interpreter." I agree with Ed. A fair system with a low, flat tax rate, no exemptions, and no Gestapo-like IRS tactics would be far better than the absurd system we have now.

154 AN ENTERPRISING LIFE

Americans may not realize how much they are really being taxed. If there were some way to educate Americans as to the extent and magnitude of federal taxation, the popular momentum necessary to vote tax-and-spenders out of office could be achieved. It may not be an accident that Election Day comes almost exactly six months after April 15, as far apart on the calendar as possible. What if Americans voted the same day they paid taxes? Also, we might revoke the federal withholding on personal income taxes. Let's all write out one check to the IRS on November 1 instead of having the money withheld from our paychecks and held (without interest) by the government.

But that's only half the story. Even if we fix the tax code, we'll still have to watch our wallets because the government has other ways to take your money.

CHAPTER 14

Taxes by Another Name

For decades, Amway marketed vitamins in a box. Then the Consumer Product Safety Commission ordered us to put a childproof latch on the box. We surveyed our consumers and found they opened the latch and never closed it again, to avoid the hassle. The latch cost us fifty cents apiece, and we sell the boxes by the millions each year. Do the math and you can see how government regulation is costing you and me millions of dollars a year. It might also be killing us.

My friend Ed Feulner, president of the Heritage Foundation, wrote that the regulation requiring the latch, the Poison Prevention Packaging Act, might have easily done more harm than good. "The reason is simple," Ed wrote. "Many elderly patients hampered by a variety of crippling diseases and infirmities find it difficult to open [medicine] containers. Thus, they don't take needed medication." One pharmacist told him of older customers who had tried using pliers, hammers, screwdrivers, and hand-operated can openers to get the bottles open. One man stated that stomping on his bottle worked. Another woman claimed that her seven-year-old granddaughter could open her bottle when she, herself, could not. They might as well have named the legislation the "Proper Packaging Prevention Act," for that's what it really was.

This is a wonderful illustration of the Law of Unintended Consequences. Decisions made by government often have unforeseen long-term, indirect consequences. By attempting to stamp out every small hazard, government regulators can essentially back away from one problem and into another. For instance, safety regulators insisted that children's night clothing be made flame retardant, only to find out later that the chemical used to treat the fabric may cause cancer. As I write this, there is substantial debate over federally mandated air bags in automobiles—the explosive force has been known to kill small adults, children, and even unborn babies. Bureaucrats may be killing us, and our children, with their "kindness."

What government regulation generally fails to acknowledge is that people can usually look out for their own interests better than a distant bureaucrat can, and at far lower cost. We are overburdening the public with layers and layers of costs, first with taxes to support the huge government bureaucracies that administer these thousands of laws, and then with higher prices that are necessary to support all of the nonproductive activities necessary to comply with the laws. If Americans were faced with the real price tag for all these regulations, I believe most consumers would say "Forget it, I'll take my chances." Regulation can be like a particularly evil form of taxation. The government says it is necessary to keep business from hurting people. In truth, it prevents business from *helping* people. Through regulation, individuals and businesses can be saddled with thousands of useless rules and regulations, which typically result in slowing down the economy. Millions of people have been taken out of productive, wealth-producing work and turned into faceless bureaucrats. These armies of bureaucrats divert the businessman's attention from the legitimate and necessary work of giving better goods and services to his customers at lower prices. Businessmen spend many, many useless hours each year filling out forms in an unproductive and costly legal confrontation with governmental agencies.

Americans have forgotten the wise words of James Madison, who warned of the dangers of heavy regulation:

> It will be of little avail to the people that the laws are made by men of their own choice if the laws be so voluminous that they cannot be read, or so incoherent that they cannot be understood; if they be repealed or revised before they are promulgated, or undergo such incessant changes that no man, who knows what the law is today, can guess what it will be like tomorrow.

How does the regulatory burden compare with the tax burden? The Tax Freedom Day—the date each year when the average American, if starting the year working only to pay taxes, would finally be free to earn income for himself—is one way of noticing just how much of our productive life goes to paying taxes. In 1902 Tax Freedom Day fell on January 31. Twenty-three years later the tax burden had crept forward only slightly to February 6. Then came the Great Depression, and with the depression came hundreds of government programs. In 1930 Tax Freedom Day stood at February 13, and over the next fifteen years it marched forward into each taxpayer's year, until in 1945 taxpayers were working for Uncle Sam up to

April Fool's Day. This reflects an approximate doubling of the tax burden over a fifteen-year period. It took three more decades, but the date eventually made it into May in 1974. Under President Bush the Tax Freedom Day only moved ahead one day, from May 1 in 1980 to May 2 in 1988. President Clinton has presided over the most dramatic one-term change (in either direction) in Tax Freedom Day since President Johnson's administration. In 1992 Tax Freedom Day stood at April 30, while in 1997, Americans couldn't start working for themselves until May 9.

Tax Freedom Day, however, does not come close to estimating the whole of the burden placed on the American people by the federal government. Since 1865, and especially since Franklin D. Roosevelt took office in 1933, federal regulation has been sapping the strength of America, shackling business and destroying our ability to compete in the world market. The best estimate of the federal regulatory burden I know of, a study by Thomas Hopkins of the Rochester Institute of Technology, puts the cost of complying with federal regulatory law at $668 billion in 1995. Federal rules cost the average American household $7,000 in 1995, $1,000 more than their average income tax bill. As bad as this sounds, Mr. Hopkins's study is an underestimate—it only includes the costs of complying with regulatory laws for which cost studies have been done. The cost of adjusting to new regulations, for example, is omitted. If Mr. Hopkins's estimate of the burden of regulatory law were added to the tax burden, Americans would spend most of the year working for Uncle Sam.

Federal regulation can hurt not only large employers but home businesses as well. This is, of course, something we at Amway are very concerned about. So when regulators clamped down on home knitting businesses in Vermont in 1979, I was paying close attention. The U.S. Department of Labor, then under Ray Marshall, a Carter appointee, sent agents out to several homes in Vermont, where they discovered a group of women who were knitting sweaters, scarves, and ski hats without benefit of union protection. These women were selling these items for profit, which put them in violation of some obscure provisions of the Fair Labor Standards Act. These regulations prohibit the home manufacture of seven specific products, including knitted outerwear, that compete with unionized industries.

The knitters finally won, after a new Reagan-appointed labor secretary abolished the rule, but the case illustrates a major problem with regulation. What's wrong with a group of women working in their homes to produce a useful product, and why should the federal government feel the need to prevent this sort of productive behavior?

The body of regulatory law has become a massive usurpation of the sovereignty of other "spheres" of authority (to once again employ Abraham Kuyper's term). This is not a new problem. In 1840, Alexis de Tocqueville compared the young American republic with European government, which had expanded into the domains of individuals and private institutions:

> The authority of government has not only spread, as we have just seen, throughout the sphere of all existing powers, till that sphere can no longer contain it, but it goes further and invades the domain heretofore reserved to private independence. A multitude of actions which were formerly entirely beyond the control of the public administration have been subjected to that control in our time, and the number of them is constantly increasing.

This could have been written in 1998. There is indeed nothing new under the sun. But Tocqueville goes on:

It is evident that most of our rulers will not content themselves with governing the people collectively; it would seem as if they thought themselves responsible for the actions and private conditions of their subjects, as if they had undertaken to guide and to instruct each of them in the various incidents of life and to secure their happiness quite independently of their own consent. On the other hand, private individuals grow more and more apt to look upon the supreme power in the same light; they invoke its assistance in all their necessities, and they fix their eyes upon the administration as their mentor or their guide.

Government regulatory agencies act as though they believe the American people have the collective intelligence of a toadstool. Sometimes, as Tocqueville pointed out, the citizens of a nation bring it on themselves when they refuse to take responsibility for their own actions. Frequently, however, the regulations seem to be the result of a disorganized committee of incompetents. Decisions from Washington are made by men so far from the problem they don't even know the questions. An unplanned society contains better planning because the people making decisions are closest to the problem.

In the end, regulation can lead to the destruction of culture and society. After commenting on the dangers of unnecessary government intervention, Tocqueville wrote of his concern for the American people: "I do not fear that they will meet with tyrants in their rulers but rather with guardians." A government led by these men, he went on, "does not destroy, but it prevents existence; it does not tyrannize, but it compresses, enervates, extinguishes, and stupefies a people, till [they are] reduced to nothing better than a flock of timid and industrious animals, of which the government is the shepherd."

A Firm Foundation

I've taken a fair amount of heat over the years for mixing my Christian faith with my conservative economic and political views. I guess some people think it's a crime to believe in an absolute authority and then let that belief influence all areas of your life. What's really at work here, I think, is a basic distrust of business based on misconceptions and half-truths. In 1985, the essayist and editor Lewis Lapham wrote, "The genius of capitalism consists precisely in its lack of morality. Unless he is rich enough to hire his own choir, a capitalist is a fellow who, by definition, can ill afford to believe in anything other than the doctrine of the bottom line." He couldn't be more wrong, in my opinion. Too many people think it is a contradition to link the word Christian with capitalist, but I believe capitalism and free enterprise work best within the context of Judeo-Christian values. Successful entrepreneurs, though often not churchgoers, know that they cannot succeed for long through dishonesty, greed, selfishness, and sloth. That's because God did not arrange the world to penalize those who followed His commandments. There are real, this-world benefits to moral behavior, in addition to a heavenly reward.

Amway is one of a number of businesses that have taken moral stands where they may seem to be financially stupid. For instance, we have committed to shutting down our facilities completely on Sundays, even though many financial wizards would tell us that we need to be running our machines seven days a week to make the best use of our capital. Rich and I hold to the idea that God intended for humans to have a day of rest once a week, and it would be hypocritical for us to ask thousands of employees to work on that day. Not only does this day give us the opportunity for worship and the physical rest that we need; it allows us the time with family and friends that our busy lives don't always allow us. Closing on Sundays has had its costs, but in a broad sense, we think the policy has helped us. Following traditional ideas of morality has its benefits, spiritual and material.

Rich and I have preached the principles of free enterprise from the very beginning because we believe it offers the greatest opportunity for man to become what God intended. Surprisingly, not everyone at Amway shares this view. Rich once met a distributor in France who professed to be a communist.

"How can you be in Amway," Rich asked, "when the free-enterprise system Amway is based on puts the emphasis on the individual and your philosophy puts it on the state?"

Answered the Frenchman, "It's easy. I need the money."

It's baffling to me that someone who is a hard worker, like

our French distributor, would advocate a system that takes wealth from other hard workers and entrusts it to state bureaucrats. But that's yet another blessing of freedom. Our French distributor is free to believe communism, even as he makes his living on the strength of capitalism.

Another factor is at work besides the increased material success that we knew would accrue to everyone in a free society. Freedom is an ethical concept. If Amway was to be run in an ethical manner, we knew that we had to emphasize those moral principles that lead to a free society. Each person who enjoyed success in Amway owed that success to God, whether they recognized it or not. It is by God's grace that we have freedom in this great nation, and it is by God's grace that we will continue to have freedom. Only a society established upon the solid moral principles found in the Bible will be a truly free society. In holding this opinion we consider ourselves to be in good company—early-American society was based on this very idea. In 1797, George Washington said in his farewell address that "of all the dispositions and habits which lead to political prosperity, religion and morality are indispensable supports."

Without the stability of a Christian moral and ethical consensus, a society of liberty can easily become a society of libertines. If the criterion for good is that which feels good, then our society becomes hedonistic and destroys itself from within. An atheistic society denies God's creation of mankind, denies purpose in life, denies an ultimate reward for good and punishment for evil, destroys respect for human life, and eliminates moral integrity. Yet the world in which we live is losing the moral consensus that holds human society together.

It came as a surprise to many people that Rich and I, as Christian businessmen, would make mention of the moral decline at Amway distributor meetings. In a society that increasingly rejects anything that smacks of traditional faith and morals, we were sharply criticized for the evangelistic tone that many Amway rallies took on. It is true that no business can be religious in the sense that individuals can be religious, but many Amway distributors agreed that it would not be improper to invite ministers and other religious speakers to rallies and other events. Amway was the subject of a lot of carping and fault-finding for this stand, but Rich and I saw our faith as inseparable from the way we conducted business.

Sometimes, however, the rallies began to lose their original business focus. At times, we had to rein in distributors who wanted to turn what was a business meeting into a religious crusade, and the distributors who insisted on using rallies only to show off their fine clothes and jewelry. A sense of balance was needed. A business gives everyone an opportunity to live out their calling, provide for their families, and contribute to worthy causes. But in the absence of Christian virtue, the attainment of wealth is nothing more than a distraction from eternal things.

As Amway gained a higher profile, the free-enterprise emphasis and the traditional religious tone of some of our meetings made us a target for statists, theological liberals, and atheists. Liberal journalists, columnists, talk-show hosts, and anyone else with a disdain for conservative ideas took potshots at us. It's not as though we excluded people from Amway because of their political or religious views. Like the communist French distributor Rich met, all sorts of people have found success through Amway. But in our judgment, the Amway system of business (and every other business) flourished best under a moral free-enterprise system. The political left-wingers wanted to curtail the free-enterprise system, and the theological left-wingers didn't understand how capitalism could possibly be compassionate or moral.

We were able by the seventies to make large contributions to conservative organizations, the Republican Party, and a few individual political campaigns, which irked the liberals to no end. But our political contributions and other activities were simply a matter of survival. The independent entrepreneur operating in a free-enterprise system was an endangered species, and Rich and I were going to fight for his protection. Sometimes that fight took us to the highest levels of government.

CHAPTER 16

Always a Republican?

When Ronald Reagan took office in 1981, I expected to see massive reductions in the regulatory burden over the next several years. Unfortunately, Congress managed to sabotage many of the Reagan administration's plans, and many conservatives didn't get the results they were expecting. By the end of 1982, a lot of overregulation was still in place— there were just about as many forms to fill out and rules to comply with in most industries. There was, at least, a different attitude on the part of the people who were doing the regulating. But industry was still dealing with the same basic regulatory structure.

The rate of increase of the regulatory burden did decline

substantially during the Reagan administration. In my speeches for the U.S. Chamber of Commerce, I noted that during the Carter administration new regulatory laws for the United States were coming out at the rate of a thousand pages a week, or fifty thousand pages a year. Even the lawyers who make it their business to know federal regulations couldn't keep up with all of that. The Reagan administration cut this to just a few pages per week.

The Reagan administration also did a great job of communicating conservative ideas to the American people. Average people embraced these ideas in 1980 and again in 1984 because they saw in them a solution to perilous economic policies. Even though Reagan was not successful in overcoming the deficit problem, he did a very good job of educating people about its dangers. Reagan lacked the tools to overcome the deficit, but he understood the perils of running an economy on debt. If Congress had been on his side, we might have obtained a smaller, balanced budget.

In 1984, at the end of Reagan's first term, American entrepreneurs formed 635,000 new businesses, an all-time high and a staggering 19 percent increase over 1980. "An opportunity society awaits us," said President Reagan that year. "We need only believe in ourselves and give men and women of faith, courage, and vision the freedom to build it." This contagious "can do" philosophy struck a chord with Americans of all political persuasions, and the result was fantastic growth.

All this growth was not limited to upper-income groups, as Reagan's opponents claimed. In 1984, the investment-driven recovery produced the sharpest one-year decline in the poverty rate in eleven years. The Bureau of the Census reported that the number of Americans at or below the poverty income line declined by 1.8 million people that year, positive proof that Reagan's prescriptions were working. In an editorial, the *Detroit News* reported that this drop was "the fullest vindication of Mr. Reagan's thesis that it is economic growth, not social spending, that really fights poverty." And you wonder why I'm a Ronald Reagan fan?

MEETING THE PRESIDENT

Rich and I first met Ronald Reagan during his 1980 presidential campaign. As Reagan began making more progress in the primaries, he went down to Palm Springs to get advice from President Ford. During their conversation, Ford mentioned Rich and me and told Reagan that he needed to meet us. So Bill Casey, who was working the Reagan campaign after the New Hampshire primary, called John Gartland in Amway's Washington, D.C., office. John was able to set up a date for us to meet Reagan in his L.A. office.

Rich and I both were quickly impressed with Reagan. After the decade of the seventies, which had produced a damaged economy and new lows in morale, Americans needed a man like Reagan to rebuild confidence in their country. We talked with Reagan at some length and encouraged him to choose George Bush for vice president and Alexander Haig for secretary of state, which of course he did.

After this visit, Rich and I decided to orchestrate an independent campaign to express our support for Ronald Reagan's candidacy. Of course, we could not spend corporate money or employ our distributors to support his candidacy, but we did what we could do. We purchased ads at our own personal expense, with our photos, and placed them in newspapers around the country expressing our support for Reagan.

President Reagan and I were able on occasion to meet in the Oval Office. The Oval Office is surprisingly small considering the station of its occupant, but it is richly decorated to reflect America's colonial history and the tastes of the president. In the Reagan years the room only accommodated a few pieces of furniture—two couches facing one another, separated by a mahogany coffee table, in front of Reagan's massive wooden desk. The desk had a neat, uncluttered look, suggesting that Reagan did not actually spend much time behind it. Behind the desk was a credenza bearing framed pictures and memorabilia not much different from what might adorn a corporate president's office. The expansive White House lawn was visible through large bulletproof windows framed with heavy green curtains.

I recall sitting down with Reagan on the couches there in the Oval Office and discussing leadership techniques. We were served coffee by a navy steward and left alone to talk. Reagan had been having some problems getting the whole truth from some of his staff, a problem I had faced not too long before. The president of the United States and the head of a large corporation can face the same difficulties—both are beset with people trying to provide information that is always a little slanted toward their point of view. Anyone in high office has to have good, trustworthy lieutenants, but it's important to have a wide variety of information sources no matter who the lieutenants are. Otherwise, we run the risk of finding ourselves isolated, unable to get consistent, reliable information. This opens us up to subtle manipulation by those surrounding us. Bias in reporting is always present, I said; the trick is to detect it before it causes problems. So I told Reagan about my system of using three unrelated sources of information. Each source of information is matched up with the other two sources to confirm it. Each person who reports to me sees things from their particular perspective. Three sources of information are usually sufficient to get a complete picture of the situation, enough to make a much more intelligent decision.

I supported Reagan on the vast majority of his policies, but there were occasions when I had to stand up to him in an effort to keep him from making a mistake. About the third year of

Reagan's administration, he was persuaded by some of his staff that a tax increase was necessary to cut the deficit. The then-chairman of the Chamber of Commerce was called to the White House to discuss the matter, and he came away supporting the tax increase. At the time, I was the head of the Executive Committee at the chamber, and I flatly refused to go along with the tax increase. With Tom Donohue (my close friend who is currently the president of the U.S. Chamber of Commerce) I led the opposition to the tax increase among the chamber board. Before long, Reagan called, from on board *Air Force One*. For forty-five minutes we went back and forth over the tax increase, he trying to convince me that it was a necessary evil, and I trying to persuade him to try further spending cuts instead. Neither of us budged. I think it pained Reagan to push for higher taxes, but he had to go by what he thought was best for the economy at the time, and so did I.

THE NEXT PRESIDENT?

The Reagan days are long gone now, but many Americans would like to see a revival of the principles of limited government and monetary responsibility. However, neither major political party seems capable of putting forth a presidential candidate who stands for these principles and who is able to communicate them effectively to the American people.

The ideal candidate will firmly defend lower taxes, less spending on needless government programs, and freer international trade. He will understand the need for dramatically reduced regulation and will be willing to actually eliminate unnecessary and unconstitutional government agencies. He will be a man of integrity, steadfast on moral issues, faithful to his own wife and children, and uncompromising on his sound ethical principles. The candidate will stand for the freedom of the individual and the family and will favor a return to strict constitutional limitations on the power and scope of the federal government. Finally, once in office, the president will not waver on his principles or go back on his promises.

If the candidate is right, it doesn't much matter to me which political party supports him. Even though I have given extensively to the Republican Party, my allegiance is to principles, not any one party. Political parties come and go, and their platforms are subject to change without notice. When I walk into a polling booth on Election Day, I see before me the names of candidates for federal, state, and local offices, each with a label—usually Republican or Democrat. Often the labels are helpful. They serve the same purpose as a brand name or a trademark. Sometimes, however, the distinctions between the parties become blurred, and the label "Republican" or "Democrat" loses its value to the voter. There are Republicans who support higher government spending and believe they should be the tax collectors for the welfare state, and there are a few Democrats who truly believe in limited government and economic freedom and growth. The two parties clearly have tendencies in one direction or the other, but neither party demonstrates a consistent commitment to one unchanging set of principles.

Perhaps this is why the number of American voters who consider themselves "independent" has been increasing steadily over my lifetime. The less important party distinctions become, the fewer people will bother belonging to (or voting for) one party over another. Both major political parties have become ideologically sloppy—weak on even the important planks in the party platform and inconsistently adopting the ideas and rhetoric of the so-called opposition. With choices such as these, it's no wonder that more individual voters today are refusing to vote straight party tickets, selecting instead candidates from both major parties and even from third parties.

There are two basic competing political philosophies in the world today. The first is that the civil government should have more power and more control over our lives and our material goods, and the second is that the government should have less of that power and control. In the United States, we should expect our two major political parties to reflect that distinction.

Which of the two major parties will maintain a low-tax, small-government philosophy in the future? It may seem that the Republican Party has a lock on this position, but some prominent Republicans have recently espoused higher taxes and larger government budgets and have supported some of the Clinton administration's liberal programs. And though the Democrats are currently following the big-government philosophy, the party could conceivably return to the limited-government, low-tax principles of Thomas Jefferson, Andrew Jackson, and the pre-1932 Franklin D. Roosevelt.

And if that happens, you might witness a miracle taking place in a certain polling booth in Ada, Michigan.

CHAPTER 17

The Businessman as Environmentalist

The public has often perceived those of us in business as inherently misanthropic, wasteful, and self-centered. Being cast as the villain is nothing new for entrepreneurs. We've always had our detractors. But stereotyping us as evil exploiters of the environment is both unfair and ignorant. Some people refuse to listen to our point of view; they often have a "don't bother me with the facts" attitude.

I recall that we once sent one of our chemists—a man with a

lifetime of experience in chemistry—to a meeting in Wisconsin having to do with phosphates in detergents. During his presentation a highly excited woman screamed at him from the floor: "But we can't believe you—you're from business!" A specialist sent by the Soap and Detergent Association to a meeting in Suffolk County, New York, received a more severe treatment. The county was about to adopt an ordinance banning the sale of all detergents, and a number of representatives of interested environmental and consumer organizations were present. He received such a verbal tongue-lashing of four-letter words from these people that he vowed never again to subject himself to such insults by testifying at any such meeting.

Accusations are easy to make, and they are often quite destructive. In the rare case when we are given the opportunity to defend ourselves against these cheap shots, it is usually very expensive. A small group of university students once published a list of the alleged phosphate content of detergents with the intent that it would dissuade consumers from using those listed with high phosphate content. The list was accepted without question by the press and printed in literally thousands of publications all over the United States and Canada. It found its way into magazines, organization bulletins, and even books. It was taken as gospel truth by millions who saw it. Yet it was so full of errors that if any businessman had printed such information he could have been fined and perhaps even jailed. The list persisted for years—long after the group of students who compiled this erroneous information had disbanded.

Even the government is guilty of spreading such damaging misinformation (perhaps I should not be so surprised). The Federal Water Quality Commission once printed a list of the phosphate content of detergents and gave it to the press. I can't vouch for the products of other companies, but their figures were flat wrong on four out of five of ours. Yet the only way we could answer this false accusation by the very government bureaucrats we support with our tax money was to advertise a correction in paid ads in two hundred newspapers. And of course the credibility of a paid ad against a government publication is doubtful. We eventually received two letters from the agency admitting error in an oblique way, but no public apology or correction was provided. If I as a businessman make untrue statements about my competitors, I am subject to being sued. But government bureaucrats seem to be able to say almost anything and are insulated not only from responsibility for their errors but also from the ballot box.

Much of the ecological doomsday talk is purveyed by those who don't really believe that God rules the universe. Man has the responsibility, of course, to husband the earth's resources with care. He is going to have to continue to use all the aggregate mental capacity of the human race in using and reusing the earth's resources to satisfy his needs. He may even have to work harder to get the same results. Just as he thinks he has found new ways to give him more leisure and less work, he'll probably find he has to work harder to extract the resources to support the new and more efficient systems.

Amway started out in 1959 with one product—Liquid Organic Concentrate (or LOC All-Purpose Cleanser). The wonderful thing about LOC was that it was a leader in eliminating negative environmental impacts from cleaners. Younger people will not remember the huge piles of billowing suds that used to appear on the surface of rivers and streams as a result of hard-base or branched-chain detergent molecules. It was not uncommon to see suds piling up on the ground outside one's house under outdoor faucets. Amway was probably the very first company of any size to market biodegradable detergents. Any products that we manufactured that might find their way into the ground or surface waters had rapid biodegradable properties built in. LOC was a nonphosphate cleaner too, which helped keep the lakes and streams free from entrophication, the choking of surface waters from massive growth of algae.

It took the major soap manufacturers nearly ten years to produce and sell similar nonphosphate detergents, and only then after several states had passed rigorous environmental laws prohibiting the use of phosphates.

Because Amway was ahead of the industry in developing nonphosphate cleaners, the laws that were passed mandating nonphosphate products didn't affect us as much. We paid close attention to the legislation, however. Environmental regulation has a way of expanding rapidly—the laws that don't affect us today could easily ruin us tomorrow. What we observed was a senseless bureaucratic process that can destroy firms almost overnight and can do far more damage to the environment than an unregulated industry does.

Some firms were able to produce nonphosphate cleaners, but this was accomplished only by substituting other ingredients that may be more harmful to human health and the environment than phosphates. Of course, the bureaucrats focused only on phosphate reduction, and they neglected to consider the damage to the environment that could be done by using alternatives. Legislative action was taken before all the facts were known, and the solution became worse than the problem. People were listening to media horror stories and weren't paying attention to the truth. They were so sure that the soap industry was trying to feather its own nest that industry scientists were ignored. Immediate action was demanded.

People seem to forget that free markets can and do come up with ways to reduce pollution. In fact, the less a nation acknowledges free markets and private property, the more likely it is to have severe pollution problems. A case in point is the environmental devastation of the eastern European countries after decades of communist rule. The United Nations' Global Environmental Monitoring Program found that pollution in these nations "is among the worst on the Earth's surface." Eighty percent of the rivers, lakes, and streams in the former East Germany are too dirty to fish in or swim in, much less drink. Air pollution in some eastern European cities is so bad that cars must use their headlights during the day. People who claim that government regulation and ownership are the answers to environmental problems should consider the filthy end of these government-controlled countries.

Even in our own country, wherever private property rights don't exist, pollution abounds. Rivers, beaches, roadsides, and many public parks are dumping grounds for unhealthy and unsightly refuse. The cleanest places are often privately owned. Well-maintained private gardens, often open to the public, are prime examples of the cleansing effects of private property. Situated near Franklin D. Roosevelt's vacation home in Warm Springs, Georgia, are the beautiful Callaway Gardens, a natural paradise bursting with thriving plant and animal species. In Grand Rapids are the Frederick Meijer Gardens, which preserve attractive green acreage in a heavily populated area.

This is God's earth, created by him as a temporary home for mankind. He intended that we should use it, and we are so created that we must use the earth to support our physical existence. From it must come all of our material welfare—most of it extracted with human energy and brainpower. But to waste it, to destroy it without need, is to fling God's gift back in his face. That is exactly what socialist environmental planning does. In contrast, a political-legal system that allows people to enjoy the fruits of their labor, to receive the return of their investment in the environment, will make the most of our natural resources and reduce unnecessary pollution.

Man is not an intruder, a trespasser, upsetting the ecological balance of the earth. The earth was created with all man's uses of it in mind. Man was given dominion over the animals and commanded by God to fill and subdue the earth. This is not an outdated Christian ethic—God never rescinded that decree. Man was not an afterthought in God's creation. The world without man would be like a house without occupants. On earth, man does not disrupt the natural order of things; he is the natural order of things.

Rich and I have long felt an obligation to work with both the local and the international community to enhance the quality of human life and improve the environment. From the very first bottle of Liquid Organic Concentrate that Amway sold in 1959, we have sought to maintain a product line that is both satisfying to the consumer and low impact on the environment. Many of our products are sold in concentrated form, which reduces waste packaging and also lowers Amway's transportation and storage costs. We have always wished to be a good neighbor to those in the Grand Rapids area, and with this in mind, our manufacturing facilities and processes are designed to minimize the impact on local watersheds and the atmosphere.

As Amway matured as a company and continued to grow internationally in the 1980s, Rich and I and a few dedicated corporate officers and managers began to use our financial strength to make a difference in international environmental projects. The first big project, one that would lead us into related environmental work in the future, was a 1989 expedition to the North Pole called Icewalk.

Icewalk featured eight team members from seven countries, led by explorer Robert Swan, who tramped five hundred miles to the North Pole on foot and on skis. Besides meeting their goal of becoming the first team to walk to the North Pole, the team members presented the world with an opportunity to dramatize the importance of preserving the pristine Arctic environment. We provided almost all the funds for the expedition, which gained for Amway the respect and admiration of the world. Amway also sponsored an Icewalk Student Expedition of twenty-two young people from fifteen different countries. For our efforts with Icewalk and efforts to build awareness of environmental issues worldwide, Amway was awarded the prestigious United Nations Environment Programme's Environmental Achievement Award on World Environment Day in 1989.

The same day marked the inauguration of the Masters of the Arctic—Art in Service of the Earth exhibition at the United Nations General Assembly in New York. This unprecedented display of Inuit (Eskimo) art, which promoted worldwide respect for the culture of circumpolar peoples, became the centerpiece of Amway's environmental awareness program.

We got involved in Arctic art through my friend Bill Nicholson. Bill was in Aspen on one of his frequent ski trips and saw some pieces of Inuit sculpture sitting on the shelves at an art gallery there. The gallery director told Bill that the United Nations was planning a major exhibit of this Inuit art in New York City, and they needed a corporate sponsor. So Bill, quite impressed with the quality and uniqueness of the carvings, talked to Casey Wondergem, our public affairs director, and Casey met with the UN's Dr. Noel Brown in New York. After talking with the UN, Casey called Stuart Silver, formerly design director of the Metropolitan Museum of Art, to ask him to design an art exhibit for the UN headquarters based on the type of pieces Bill saw in Aspen. In March of 1989 he and his associates began the process of creating a world-class art exhibit. In the process, we sought out circumpolar artists to contribute more art and expanded the exhibit considerably.

The opening of the Masters of the Arctic art gallery at the UN General Assembly Building on World Environment Day, June 5, 1989, was followed by such accolades from the public and UN officials that we decided to give the gallery structure to the UN as a gift. Designed to be portable, the exhibit then began a tour of the world that continues to this day. Dr. Christopher

Stephens was persuaded to leave his curatorial job at the Yellowknife Museum to help curate the traveling exhibit. Though Masters of the Arctic remains under the auspices of the United Nations Environment Programme, the exhibit has since 1990 been the main project of the Amway Environmental Foundation, which was formed to promote and support environmental education projects for adults and children worldwide. We received requests from all over the world to display the Masters of the Arctic exhibit. Over the next few years the art show traveled to Washington, D.C., and Dallas, and then to Canada, Mexico, Japan, Brazil, and Argentina. Along the way the exhibit and Amway picked up several high honors for developing environmental awareness through indigenous art. Two years after winning the UNEP Achievement Award, we received the 1991 National Wildlife Federation National Conservation Achievement Award in the corporate leadership category. In 1992 we received the Transpolar Medal from the UN Educational, Scientific, and Cultural Organization, the United Earth Certificate of Commendation, and the Rainforest Alliance Award. In Rio de Janeiro the Masters of the Arctic show was the cultural centerpiece of the 1992 Earth Summit. It was ironic to me to hear the prime minister of Canada saying wonderful things about Amway at Rio and up in Toronto and in the Museum of Civilization in Ottawa. Just a few years earlier one would have thought, from the comments of some Canadian politicians, that Amway had been planning an overthrow of the Canadian government. Now, it seems, art has helped to heal the wounds between Amway and the Canadian government. By demonstrating our high regard for the accomplishments of the Inuit people of northern Canada, we engendered the respect of the Canadians and the rest of the world.

Corporate philanthropy can make a real difference by supporting good artists and educating people on environmental issues and the importance of sound environmental science.

Again, government involvement is superfluous and even counterproductive at times. What makes private funding even better is that it comes without the bureaucratic red tape and the political nonsense that steers government-funded art and science off in a wrong direction.

CHAPTER 18

The Home Team

I f there is one regret I have about the years I spent building Amway with Rich, it is that I didn't get to spend as much time with my children as I wanted. As much as the business has given to our family, it has taken away, too. Usually I would leave for work about nine in the morning and not return until about six o'clock. From six until dinnertime, Betty and I would spend some time together. After dinner, I would often have to go back to work. So during a lot of the kids' growing-up years, I was physically absent, leaving many of the responsibilities to Betty.

It's difficult to attain a good balance between work and time with the family. As I've observed other people in business struggle with this problem, I've come to the conclusion that it is one of the most common and greatest challenges people in business ever face. It was no less a challenge for me than for anyone else. Though the business needed most of my time early in its development, there came a point in my life when I could afford to enjoy more leisure time. Time is a resource, like a new machine or a skilled employee. It was hard for me to know when to devote that resource to the business and when to begin devoting more of it to my family.

Dinnertime sometimes provided the setting for the time I shared with the children. It was very important in the Van Andel household for us all to be home for dinner. Each meal would start with family devotions. After reading the Bible, we would discuss what it meant to us and how it applied in our lives. It's amazing how many different issues the Bible touches on, and how it can speak to us even in our modern society.

After our discussion of the passage of Scripture, I would end with a prayer. My family is probably the largest audience to have heard me pray. Prayer is, to me, a very personal conversation with God. For the sincere Christian, it is an integral part of human life. It can be something as simple as "Dear Father, please get this airplane off the ground safely," or something more lengthy when wrestling with a severe crisis. I've never done much public prayer—there is a temptation when praying before other people to grandstand, to pray for the human listeners instead of to the heavenly Listener. When my children heard me pray, however, they learned how to communicate with God, and they learned that even their dad needed his Father's strength each day. While each family's traditions are different, I know that the habit of daily prayer is now part of each of my children's families.

Perhaps most important in a child's moral and ethical development is the example set by their parents in daily living. When one's home life is not pleasing to God, it is worse than useless to put on a front of good behavior for the outside world.

Our conversations around that dinner table were a big part of our family life together, and topics ranged from the business to our faith to politics and economics. They were often simple conversations, frequently interrupted by some telephone call or a teenage child's dashing out the door to some all-important meeting with friends. But that limited time was used to change my children's lives. Only now, as I observe with great joy the lives of all four of my children, do I realize what blessings God can bestow on time spent together as a family over the dinner table.

Sometimes the dining room took on the character of an MBA classroom. As I would reflect on the day's activities, I would present the family with a business problem and start a discussion of the various solutions. Then I'd tell everyone what I actually did in that situation, and why. Those discussions made for a much easier transition when my children and Rich's children began taking on leadership roles in Amway. Through what went on in my home and in Rich's home, our eight children had gained an understanding of what the business was all about and how to run it efficiently and well. My son Dave told me not long ago that he learned more about business around the dinner table than from any other source—college business classes and personal involvement in the business included.

OUT AND ABOUT

Like most families, we found trips to be a great way to spend time together. As you might guess, we've had some great ones—from the Great Barrier Reef in Australia to float trips down the Amazon and Colorado Rivers. History lessons from school came alive as we saw the battlefield at Waterloo, drove down the Appian Way in Italy, and walked the beach in the Philippines where General Douglas MacArthur waded ashore in 1944.

Sometimes, the less glamorous experiences were more memorable. We used to camp at a place we owned in northern Michigan that had an outhouse. Not an ordinary outhouse, mind you. This one had a gas-fired unit that took whatever was deposited and neatly incinerated it. For several years, it worked just fine. One summer, however, about halfway through our vacation, the outhouse began to malfunction. So the kids mentioned it to me, Mr. Fix-It. The next day, I decided to look it over just before I had to leave for a Chamber of Commerce speaking engagement. Now, this was in the early 1970s, and I happened to be wearing a beautiful pair of white polyester pants and a white polyester shirt. It wouldn't take but a minute or two to fix, I thought, so I stepped into the outhouse and began fiddling around with it. I couldn't figure out what was wrong, so I gave up, turned around, and dropped the lid behind me.

Steve and Dave had been out fishing and were just pulling the boat up to the dock when the unthinkable happened. In a normally functioning outhouse of this sort, dropping the lid ignites the gas that burns the waste. But some gas had leaked out and accumulated in the enclosed area, and when I dropped the lid, the outhouse exploded. Steve and Dave described hearing a loud boom and watching splinters, smoke, and everything else go flying fifty feet into the air. Then they saw their father, now wearing white polyester shorts and a white polyester T-shirt, staggering away from the remains of the outhouse. My hair was askew, my eyebrows singed, and smoke was slowly rising from my back.

Betty ran out of the RV and, not knowing what else to do, frantically hosed me down with Am-Medic, Amway's antiseptic spray. Except for my singed eyebrows and a ringing in the ears, I was fine, but the next summer we had an electric-fired outhouse.

Most of our summers were not marked by exploding outhouses, however, and we enjoyed wonderful times together as a family. The impact on my children was obvious—while enjoying the outdoors, they learned to appreciate the beauty of God's creation, and they learned to cooperate with other members of the family in our various activities together.

THE NURSERY OF SOCIETY

Many parents, in their efforts to change our society for the better, forget that the most powerful tool for social change is the home. It's not high schools, it's not science, it's not technology, it's not the arts, and it's not even government. If you want to improve society, look to your own house, fathers and mothers!

The great Puritan preacher Cotton Mather once exhorted his congregation to look after their own families if they desired to be of service to people around them. "Families are the Nurseries of all Societies," Mather said.

No political action committee, no political party, no president has as much power to change society as the institution of the family. A stronger family structure means a lower crime rate, a more effective "social safety net" for individuals in crisis, and a more virtuous society. When two parents (or more often in today's world a single parent) raise their children to do what is right, they contribute to everyone else's welfare. No big government can truly appreciate the value of each child—their strengths and weaknesses, their talents and natural inclinations. Each child is a unique individual, and each requires the special love and wisdom of a parent. I know that was the case in our household. With each child came new and different challenges, and Betty and I had to adapt to each one.

THE PATHBREAKER

Nan, our eldest, was the first of my children to begin working at Amway. She started out in the unglamorous internal auditing department and then went to personnel. Rich and I eventually decided to set up a management training program for our children, and Nan and Dick DeVos were the guinea pigs, in some sense. Our philosophy was to let them learn the ropes from the inside rather than letting them work for another company first. We didn't start them at the top; the kids worked in just about every part of Amway, doing all kinds of jobs. Nan was on the soap lines, loading the skids, filling the lines with bottles, and learning to deal with people at all levels in the company. I wanted her to understand how vital every job, every person, is in Amway. That way, when she entered higher-level management, she would be a more effective leader and communicator. "It's kind of fun working out there," she says. "The nice thing about it is, you go to work, you do your job, and you leave your job behind at the end of the day." But of course Nan moved out of that phase of her training into Amway's expanding communications department and became a vice president in 1984. She is now in charge of all Amway printed materials, audiovisuals, and speeches, including our monthly magazine for Amway's North American distributors and catalog development.

Nan has always been concerned about the inclusion of women in the American corporate environment, and she has spoken out eloquently and often on women's issues. Nan's actions match her words—her civic involvement has been directed toward those activities that deal with "helping women achieve economic independence," as she says. Nan is involved with Hope Community, a local shelter for homeless women and families in crisis, and Grand Rapids Opportunities for Women, a program that trains low- and middle-income women to be entrepreneurs. "If you believe in something, then you'd better live your own life that way," Nan says.

Nan also keeps busy by working with other local and national groups, including the Grand Rapids Art Museum, the

Republican Women's Forum, the Michigan State Chamber of Commerce, and the American Mensa Society. She has always been willing to give her time to as many charitable organizations as she can, and she has helped to raise millions of dollars for groups such as Easter Seals, the YWCA Sexual Abuse Treatment Center, the United Way, and Goodwill. "I could have been born in a gutter in Calcutta or a field in Ethiopia," she says. "The position and circumstance to which I was born, I feel, obligated me to other people."

Of her work at Amway, she says, "I'll stay as long as God wants me here and as long as I'm happy. I love what I do; I can't imagine doing anything else. I believe very much in what we do and why we do it."

AN INDEPENDENT MIND

My eldest son, Steve, who is now chairman of Amway, wasn't always sure he wanted to follow in his father's footsteps. Steve went through a brief period of soul-searching during which he looked at all the options available to him. After a year or two of examining all the possibilities, Steve reached the point where he was ready to work for Amway. He entered the management training program that Rich and I had set up and became thoroughly committed to the development and success of Amway.

During Steve's teenage years, we went through some rocky times in our relationship. Steve was growing up into a fine young man, but there were times when he needed boundaries. Just like most teenagers, Steve would sometimes test those boundaries. It took time for Steve to grow into responsibility, to find his place in life. For me, it was an exercise in obedience to Proverbs 19:18: "Chasten your son while there is hope, and do not set your heart on his destruction."

A failure to "chasten" a son, then, can result in terrible consequences for him. I think the chastening that the proverb mentions takes different forms as children grow older. When Steve was sixteen, one particular incident fundamentally changed our relationship and the way I worked to train and guide him. I had grounded him for two weeks for some infraction of the household rules. Steve decided that he had been treated unjustly and that he was not going to be stuck at home while his friends were out having fun. So one night he took his car and went out. I didn't say anything to him, but before I went to work early the next morning I took his car keys off the kitchen counter and slipped them into my pocket.

Steve woke up a couple of hours later and searched around for his keys. It finally dawned on him what had happened. In a fit of rebellion, he called a friend to come over and pick him up, without telling anyone where he was going. He spent the night over at the friend's house and came back the next day.

Betty and I were pretty concerned. Betty hadn't seen Steve leave, and we had no idea where he might have gone. When Steve came back, I gave him his keys and said, "Look, if you're going to go out and stay out, I'd just as soon you be in control, you be driving. I won't ground you ever again. I only ask that you come and talk to me if you want to do something or have any questions. You're old enough now to make your own decisions, but at least give me the opportunity to give my opinion." At that point I think my relationship with Steve changed. No longer would I treat him as a young child. He was growing into adulthood and was going to have to take responsibility for his own actions. I would not dictate his comings and goings as one does with small children. Now my role was advisor and counselor.

Steve really appreciated that approach and told me so years later. I wouldn't recommend that strategy for every child, but for Steve, it worked. He recognized that he was being treated like an adult and would be expected to act like one. By the time Steve left for college, he had matured immeasurably, and marriage to Cindy, a wonderful young woman, completed his transition period. Steve has followed in my footsteps in assuming a position on the board of the U.S. Chamber of Commerce. Steve and Cindy have the same appreciation for the Grand Rapids community that Betty and I do and have continued the Van Andel tradition of supporting important community projects.

MY SON AT THE WHEEL

I generally allowed my children a good deal of freedom. Whenever I saw that they were misusing that freedom, I would intervene and discuss their behavior with them. Usually I would not approach the children with the idea of pushing my view on them, but I would certainly give them advice and urge them to reconsider their behavior if it was going to cause problems.

I think that way of doing things has affected the way my children work as leaders in Amway today. I've observed Dave using the same technique—he gives individuals considerably free rein and tells them, "I'm giving you the freedom to do this work the way you see fit, but at the end of the day, you're responsible for the actions you took. If I see something that is incompatible with the way we do business around here, or if there is something substantially wrong, at that point I'll intervene." Micromanagement of an employee's work is likely to produce the same sort of outcome that would result from constantly looking over a teenager's shoulder to see if they're doing things the way they should be done.

Of course, allowing children to have some freedom is not the same as being uninvolved or uninterested in their lives. Dave and I shared several common interests that opened up avenues of communication between us. One of them was automobiles. Dave learned to drive at the age of twelve. We had been driving around on some back roads on Water Island in my Jeep, and I turned to Dave and said, "Now's the time to start to learn." It was a stick shift, but Dave took to it pretty quickly, and soon he wanted to drive all the time. Dave has a love for fine cars just as I do. I still remember the first really exotic car that I bought—it was a used Maserati Gibley, red with a black interior. Unfortunately, the previous owner had abused it a bit, but it was a Maserati nonetheless. Dave thought it was really cool, and I'd take him out for a spin in it once in a while. As Dave grew older and as I expanded my automobile collection I would sometimes allow him to get behind the wheel of a Lamborghini or a Maserati or even a Ferrari, just for a little while.

I have since sold off much of my collection, and Dave has grown up and moved on to be "at the wheel" of several community interests in addition to his leadership role at Amway. Perhaps most prominently, Dave is overseeing operations and the construction of a building for the Van Andel Institute, of which he is chairman. As co-owner of the Grand Rapids Griffins, he was instrumental in bringing professional hockey to western Michigan. Dave's wife, Carol, is equally active in the community—she is on the Grand Rapids Opera board, is the chair of the Ada Christian School Foundation, and actively serves with Christian Schools International and Pine Rest.

MY LOVING DAUGHTER

With Barb, especially, as the youngest child, it has been difficult for me to take myself out of that parenting role with her. I still remember holding her little hand in mine as we crossed the street, and perhaps I still want to hold on to parenthood with Barb. The hardest day of my life was when one day Barb took her hand out of mine as we were about to cross the street. "Daddy, I'm old enough I can do it myself now," she said. With those words, I knew that a precious part of my life was gone forever.

As a teenager, Barb wasn't perfect, but she never went through a full-fledged rebellion period like some children do. Blessed with a strong conscience, Barb was likely to turn herself in if she did something wrong or to confess "with fear and trembling" if she got caught in some misbehavior. Once when Barb was sixteen, she told us she was going out to see a girlfriend but went to Ann Arbor instead. While she was gone, the worst snowstorm in the history of Michigan hit. This was the big snowstorm of 1976 that people still mention with veneration today. Worried, Betty called Barb's friend's house to make sure Barb was safe. As innocent as Barb was, she hadn't briefed her friend to cover for her.

Several hours later, Barb arrived, having driven all the way through the snowstorm from Ann Arbor. She had gotten stuck a time or two in the snow, and she was scared to death, not only because of the tongue-lashing she expected to receive when she got home but because she had confronted some real danger because of her lie. Barb meekly confessed and begged our forgiveness. I could see that her conscience had already convicted her and she was repentant, so Betty and I didn't have to say much.

Just a few years ago, Barb mentioned that incident to us again and told us how much she appreciated how we handled that situation. Many times, when our children were small, Betty and I questioned the wisdom of the thousand and one parenting decisions we had to make every day. Many times since our children have left the nest, we have wondered about our whole parenting strategy. Did we do everything we could have done? Could we have been more lenient? Should we have been more strict? Then, just when those doubts are the strongest, one of the children comes back to us and gives us some sign of their appreciation for us.

Barb has taken to heart the biblical mandate to "honor her father and mother," and as my health and Betty's health have declined, she has shown great care and concern for us. She has never lost her filial respect for her parents and has taken pains to find new ways to show it. Recently, Barb wrote tributes to both Betty and me, telling us plainly how much she loved and admired us. That tribute is something I will never forget.

What was even more precious was the tribute Barb gave to her mother. Betty's Alzheimer's had progressed so far along by the time that Barb presented her tribute that I doubted she would understand anything that was being read to her. Betty wasn't recognizing me or the children at that point, and it was very sad to think that this homage paid her would go unreceived and unacknowledged. So as we gathered there in the living room of our home that day, dear Barb told her mother in beautiful, poignant words what a blessing she had been to all of her children and what a model of faithful Christian motherhood she had been.

Then something strange and wonderful happened. Betty looked straight at Barb and said, "My loving daughter." For just a moment, God had given Betty comprehension of the gift Barb had given her and the words to show Barb her gratitude. Barb was overcome with emotion, and I was speechless. Barb had been hard on herself for not giving her mother this tribute earlier, before her illness became so severe, so this was a very meaningful and precious moment for Barb.

As with my other three children, Barb has found several ways to serve her community and her nation, including the national board of the Capital Research Center in Washington. Just recently, she joined me on the board of the Heritage Foundation, where I am proud to see her working to promote the ideals that made this country great. Barb met her husband, Rick Gaby, at Indiana University, where she earned her master's degree in business.

A NEW GENERATION OF LEADERS

Being the son or daughter of the cofounder of a large company is not easy. My children have had to deal with pressures and conflicts that I never faced. Growing up working in Amway, they were scrutinized more closely than any of the other employees. In management positions in Amway, my children, and Rich's as well, have had to work twice as hard as anyone else, and often they don't receive the credit due them. If they do well in management and the business grows, people will say, "Well, they had the business handed to them on a silver platter." If the business does not do well under their leadership, people will say, "Look, they destroyed the fine business their fathers built." The children also had to deal with the incessant questioning and doubting: "Are they here because of who their father is, or because they're qualified for the job?" Of course, they would most likely not be at Amway if it were not for my presence there. But that takes nothing away from their management abilities. Each of my children, and Rich's children, are very well qualified for the work they do with Amway, as proven by Amway's continued success under their leadership on the policy board. With Steve now as chairman and Dick DeVos as president, Amway is in extremely capable hands.

When my children and Rich's children entered Amway in a management capacity, Rich and I both had to deal with the pressures of balancing sibling equity with business concerns. The eight children had been working their way up through Amway for several years when Rich alerted me to the need to take some steps toward turning the business over to them. Management training was not enough. For as long as Amway had been in existence, Rich and I had made the major decisions, while the children had been somewhat isolated. Now it was time for them to be let in on the action. The children needed more information on the business's finances, and they needed to learn how to work together in making policy.

Our first step was to create what we called the policy council. The eight children would meet every month, with two outside people who would train them in group decision making. Each of the children took turns chairing the policy council to give them all experience in leadership. The agenda of each meeting was not as important as the process of coming to a consensus. The goal was not to immediately turn over important policy decisions to the children but to bring them to the point where they could quickly and effectively resolve problems set before them.

Eventually, Rich and I began sitting in on these monthly meetings. We began giving the children detailed financial information, and they got a say in how the business was run. The meetings changed from what were essentially practice discussion groups to important policy-forming sessions.

The importance of having a smooth transfer of leadership to the second generation became more clear to us all when, in July of 1992, Rich suffered a mild stroke. Rich was home from the hospital after only four days and made a complete recovery, but his illness underscored the necessity of giving our children more control over Amway. While Rich recovered, we dissolved the policy council and added our children to a new policy board, which included Rich and me. This meant that they would have more involvement in the day-to-day operations of the business and would be increasingly responsible for its success or failure.

Rich and I both knew that someday our partnership would draw to a close, but neither of us wanted to admit that that time had come. As solid as our partnership had been in the late 1940s when we were running Wolverine Air Service or trying to sail the Caribbean, cement had been applied to that partnership through decades of hardship and triumph, affliction and prosperity. But now it was time for our partnership to make way for a new generation.

We began to lay the groundwork for Rich's resignation. On Rich's recommendation and our joint decision, we settled upon Rich's eldest son, Dick, as the one who would succeed him as president.

Early on the morning of December 6, 1992, Rich had a serious heart attack at his home in Ada. Six days later he underwent triple bypass surgery and recovered quickly enough to be home for Christmas. I had some long talks with Rich while he was at the Cleveland Clinic recovering from his surgery. The first few days Rich was subdued, not much like his normal effervescent self. To come face-to-face with one's own mortality would be a blow to anyone. Quietly, soberly, we talked about our faith in God, about family and friends, about good old times, and about the future.

The day before Rich went home from the clinic, he made his resignation official. The preparations we had made for Dick's accession to the presidency were, as it turned out, well timed. By the time Rich became ill, Dick had become very familiar with the role he was to take. Rich and I had put the transition on course long before, and it was simply a matter of making the decision public.

I knew that it was also time for me to consider stepping down from the chairmanship. I had seen through policy board meetings that all of my children were fully capable of corporate leadership. But Rich and I could only choose one to become chairman, and it remained for me to make my recommendation.

I disliked very much having to choose among my children for the chairmanship, but it had to be done. For years, while the children were growing up, I tried to be scrupulously fair with them. Now, though I wanted to avoid favoritism at all costs, I could not be fair. Only one of my children could succeed me as chairman; the others would retain vice presidencies. It was such an onerous task for me that I even tried to get my friend Bill Nicholson to make the decision for me. He refused, however, saying that it had to be my choice and no one else's. For months I agonized over the choice, praying over it and considering the issue from every possible angle.

Finally I chose my son Steve, and he has not disappointed us at all. Steve is not a carbon copy of me—he has never seen the need to fashion his approach to management after my own. He has his own style and his own methods, and they seem to work very well in combination with Amway president Dick DeVos. In leading the day-to-day management team, Steve is a hard worker and an excellent coalition builder. With the support of people who like and trust him, Steve can make exciting things happen at Amway.

CHAPTER 19

First Love

May I share a little secret? Although I believe in the health benefits of Nutrilite products and take them every day, that's not why I am so fond of it. The real reason I like Nutrilite is that it introduced me to Betty.

My aunt was a Nutrilite customer who was housekeeper for the Hoekstra family of Grand Rapids. She suggested that the Hoekstras might be interested in buying Nutrilite products, so I called on Mrs. Hoekstra one morning in the spring of 1951. I was met at the door by her beautiful blond-haired, blue-eyed daughter, Betty. Making a Nutrilite sale suddenly became a secondary reason for my visit! I probably botched my sales presentation, but Mrs. Hoekstra decided to buy a box of Nutrilite products anyway.

My next mission, far more important than another Nutrilite sale, was to get a date with Miss Betty Jean Hoekstra. Luckily, she accepted.

Betty and I dated for only a couple of months before it became plain to me that I had found the woman with whom I wanted to share the rest of my life. She had the same sweetness of disposition and kindness of heart that characterized my mother, and she had a deep, sincere faith that inspired me to seek a closer relationship with God. No one, I was convinced, could be a better life partner than Betty. She graciously accepted my proposal, and at two o'clock on the afternoon of August 16, 1952, we were married at the Hoekstra home in Grand Rapids. I took to heart the verse from Proverbs: "He who finds a wife finds a good thing, and obtains favor from the Lord." Betty and I had perfectly compatible personalities. Believing as I do in the sovereignty of God in our lives, I know that God prepared us for each other and joined us together. He knew that only together would we be truly happy and complete. Only as a team would his will be accomplished in both our lives.

To Betty is due much credit for my own business success. As our living room became the meeting place for Nutrilite, and later, Amway meetings, Betty's gift of hospitality came out. She had an extraordinary ability to make people feel comfortable in social situations, and she fell easily into the role of household social coordinator and hostess.

Certain stages in the growth of the business took me away from Betty and the children much more than I would have liked. Sometimes I look back and think about what my priorities were then, and what they are today. I don't think anyone in the senior years of life can honestly look back and say, "You know, I really spent too much time with my family. I should have been at the office more often or traveled more frequently." To those of you reading this book who are still in your youth, I offer this humble admonition with all the feeling this Dutch heart can muster: Spend time with your family while you are young. There will never be enough time when you are old.

Jay Van Andel as an elementary school
graduate in front of his home in
Grand Rapids, Michigan, in 1937.

Mother, Nella Van Andel, and
grandfather John Vander Woude with
Jay in 1943 during his first furlough
after joining the service.

Lieutenant Jay Van Andel after
graduation from the Army Air Corps
cadet school at Yale University in 1945.

(All photos on this page are courtesy of the Van Andel family.)

The proud owners—Van Andel and
DeVos with one of their
flying school's airplanes in 1946.

At the opening on
May 20, 1947, the
Riverside Drive-Inn
was the first of its
kind in Grand
Rapids and proved a
successful sideline to
the young partners'
air service business.

Anchors aweigh: Van Andel and DeVos in winter of 1949
en route to the Caribbean aboard the 38-foot schooner
Elizabeth, which sank off the coast of Cuba.

Rich DeVos and Jay Van Andel with
the salvaged life preserver from the ill-
fated Elizabeth upon their return from
South America in July 1949.

*(All photos on this spread are
courtesy of the Van Andel family.)*

The offices and meeting room of Ja-Ri Corporation.
(*Courtesy of the Van Andel family*)

The successful entrepreneurs at the Ja-Ri Corporate Offices,
the start-up that would evolve into Amway Corporation.
(*Courtesy of the Van Andel family*)

The wedding of Betty Hoekstra and Jay Van Andel
on August 16, 1952, at Betty's family's home on
Wealthy Street in Grand Rapids, Michigan.
(*Bultman Studio*)

Jay and Rich with Early Nutrilite/Ja-Ri Distributors in California in May 1956.
(*Courtesy of the Van Andel family*)

Cozy quarters: The converted service station in Ada, Michigan, that became
Amway's first outside office building in October 1960.
(*Courtesy of Amway Corporation*)

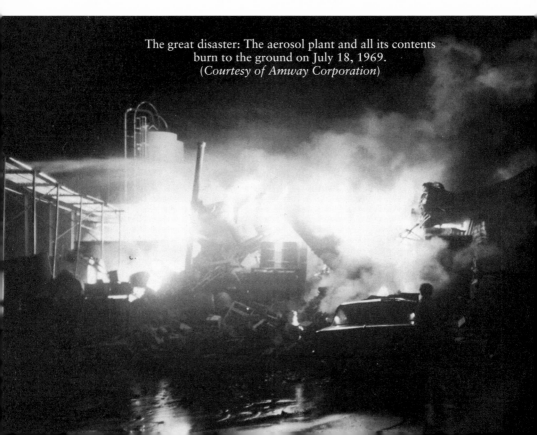

The great disaster: The aerosol plant and all its contents
burn to the ground on July 18, 1969.
(*Courtesy of Amway Corporation*)

Jay and Betty Van Andel prior to the 10th anniversary celebration of Amway Corporation in 1969. (*Courtesy of the Van Andel family*)

President Gerald R. Ford, Rich DeVos, and Jay Van Andel at the White House in 1975 discussing Grand Rapids economic development and Amway's international outreach. (*Courtesy of Amway Corporation*)

Christmas at Amway, 1980 — Jay and Betty Van Andel
with Rich and Helen DeVos.
(*Courtesy of Amway Corporation*)

Jay Van Andel, General Alexander Haig, and Rich DeVos at a 1981
press conference for the openings of the Gerald R. Ford Presidential
Museum and the Amway Grand Plaza Hotel.
(*Courtesy of Amway Corporation*)

Mstislav Rostropovich, director for the National Symphony Orchestra, with Jay and Betty Van Andel at the Amway sponsored tour of Europe in February 1982.
(*Capital Press & Photo Services B.V. the Netherlands*)

Jay Van Andel, chairman of the 1982 Netherlands-American Bicentennial Commission, and wife Betty are greeted by President Ronald Reagan at the White House reception for Queen Beatrix of the Netherlands.
(*Capital Press & Photo Services B.V. the Netherlands*)

Royal reception at Vice President George Bush's home in April 1982.
Left to right: Vice President George Bush, Prince Claus, Her Majesty Queen
Beatrix, Betty Van Andel, NABC Chairman Jay Van Andel, and Barbara Bush.
(*Capital Press & Photo Services B.V. the Netherlands*)

Jay and Betty Van Andel, Prince Claus, Congressman Guy VanderJagt, and
Her Majesty Queen Beatrix aboard a Coast Guard cutter during a trip to
Holland, Michigan, with the royal party in June 1982.
(*Capital Press & Photo Services B.V. the Netherlands*)

Untarnished image: An in-depth interview with Mike Wallace for CBS's
60 Minutes, which aired January 9, 1983.
(*Courtesy of Amway Corporation*)

Amway's co-founders
Rich DeVos and Jay Van Andel
in 1986 on the occasion of Amway's 25th Anniversary. (*Portrait by David LaClaire*)

Jay Van Andel holding the official gavel at his swearing in as Commissioner-General of the Genoa World's Fair in 1989, with Ambassador Peter Secchia.

At the dedication of the Van Andel Plaza at Hope College in Grand Rapids, Michigan, in 1990. Left to right: Rick and Barb Gaby (daughter), Jay Van Andel, Betty Van Andel, Carol and Dave Van Andel (son), and Nan Van Andel (daughter).

(All photos on this spread are courtesy of Amway Corporation.)

The Van Andel Arena in downtown Grand Rapids, dedicated in September 1996 in the names of Jay and Betty Van Andel.

Amway Corporation Policy Board. *Seated (left to right):* Richard M. DeVos, Co-founder; Steve Van Andel, Chairman; Richard M. DeVos, Jr., President; Jay Van Andel, Co-founder. *Standing (left to right):* Cheri DeVos-Vander Weide, VP Corporate Affairs; David Van Andel, Senior VP Operations; Doug DeVos, Senior VP/Managing Director Amway North America; Nan Van Andel, VP Catalog & Communications; Dan DeVos, VP Corporate Affairs; Barb Van Andel-Gaby, VP Corporate Affairs.

The Amway Corporation World Headquarters in Ada, Michigan.

(All photos on this spread are courtesy of Amway Corporation.)

Current Chairman and President
of Amway Corporation—
Second Generation: Steve Van Andel
and Dick DeVos.

The Van Andel Institute, opening in
November 1999. All funding is provided
by the Jay and Betty Van Andel Foundation.
The total building cost is estimated at $200 million.

Eagles Nest—the private residence on Peter Island.

Jay and Betty Van Andel in later years relaxing at
White Bay on Peter Island.

(Photos on this page are courtesy of Amway Corporation.)

By taking on the responsibilities inside and outside of the home that Betty did, she lightened my load and enabled me to do the work that I have done with Amway. She made a lot of sacrifices and worked just as hard as I did, for less public acclaim than I received. In God's eyes, her work as a wife, mother, hostess, and community leader is no less important than mine. For I believe that we work not for the rewards of men but for the praise of heaven. This beautiful selection from the Bible really describes the woman I married:

Who can find a virtuous wife?
For her worth is far above rubies.
The heart of her husband safely trusts her;
So that he will have no lack of gain.
She does him good and not evil
All the days of her life.
. . . She is like the merchant ships,
She brings her food from afar.
She also rises while it is yet night,
And provides food for her household,
And a portion for her maidservants.
She considers a field and buys it;
From her profits she plants a vineyard.
. . . She extends her hand to the poor,
Yes, she reaches out her hands to the needy.
. . . Strength and honor are her clothing;
She shall rejoice in time to come.
She opens her mouth with wisdom,
And on her tongue is the law of kindness.
She watches over the ways of her household,
And does not eat the bread of idleness.
Her children rise up and call her blessed;
Her husband also, and he praises her.
Many daughters have done well,

But you excel them all.
Charm is deceitful and beauty is passing,
But a woman who fears the Lord shall be praised.
Give her of the fruit of her hands,
And let her works praise her in the gates.
                                    —FROM PROVERBS 31

While I was frequently gone because of Amway-related work, Betty was always with the children. She was the stabilizing force in the home whenever I couldn't be. Whenever the kids would come home from school, they would yell "Mom!" not necessarily because they wanted to see her but just for the comfort of knowing she was there. Betty would always respond, "Yup, I'm here!"

As the children grew older, Betty began directing her energies outside the home. Locally, Betty got involved with the Opera of Grand Rapids and succeeded in getting me involved as well. The opera is now in its thirty-first anniversary year, thanks partly to my wife's work in its behalf. Betty, who had a big heart for children, was also behind the Van Andel Center for Children and Adolescents at Pine Rest Christian Hospital in Grand Rapids. On the national level, Betty was involved with Phyllis Schlafly's Eagle Forum, a conservative political organization.

Betty was never afraid to speak her mind. She had thought through a lot of issues and knew what she believed. Everyone who knew her was deeply impressed by her deep faith in God—people remarked that they couldn't talk five minutes with Betty without the subject turning to religion. That faith, which permeated and informed every part of her life, was to her the root of life. Barb remarked recently that she remembers getting up in the mornings and looking down the stairs to see her mother sitting in her favorite chair, her Bible in her lap and her hands clasped in prayer.

IN SICKNESS AND IN HEALTH

In 1988, I started to notice that Betty was having trouble remembering things. At first, it was just an occasional memory lapse—a misplaced purse, lost keys, a forgotten phone number. Then the memory lapses became more frequent, and Betty began forgetting things no well person forgets. She became easily confused and had difficulty doing simple tasks. It was hard for me to accept the fact that she was seriously ill.

Then the children began to confront me on the issue. Each one of them was deeply concerned, of course, but Barb took the lead in persuading me that Betty needed to have better medical attention. She had to get me over my deeply ingrained suspicion of the medical community and remind me that Betty's welfare was more important than my privacy. Barb and Dave helped me seek out a doctor in South Carolina who had been doing some advanced work in cases like Betty's, and he began working with her on a regular basis.

The next two years saw Betty slip very quickly. She went from having one person help her with different things during the day to having twenty-four-hour care. I would work with her to try to preserve her memory, taking her to her favorite places, showing her pictures, playing her favorite pieces of music. Sometimes she would seem to improve, but these times never lasted more than a few days. God can take even the most grievous evils in our lives and use them for his good purposes. As the Betty I knew has been taken from me through mental decay, and as my own health has deteriorated, he has brought my children back into my life in a wonderful way. My relationships with them have grown stronger as both they and I have matured. Betty's illness has forced me to turn to them for support, and they, I think, have come closer to me as we meet their mother's needs together. Now more than ever before, I treasure my children, because they are Betty's living legacy, the fruit of all her best years.

It was very difficult for me to watch this curtain come down on Betty's mind. I determined to maintain our little routines and preserve as much of her world as possible. White Bay, on Peter Island, is one of my favorite places. Lush tropical vegetation cascades down the surrounding hills to meet the narrow white beach. I take Betty down to the shore there and into the water where she is able to stand up and walk with my assistance. The water there is very calm, as the reefs at the mouth of the bay provide shelter from the force of the ocean swells. Sometimes we will spend an hour or more there, just walking back and forth, until she tires and is ready to return to her beach chair. It's good physical exercise for both of us, and varied experiences are good for Betty's mind. The most gratifying reward for me comes when Betty blesses me with one of her smiles, which even in illness have not faded. I stay with Betty as much as I can, keeping her company. I don't begrudge her the time—it's a joy to me to have the opportunity to give something back to her in return for all the compromises she made for me during those years of building Amway. If marriage vows were kept only as long as acts of service could be reciprocated, marriage wouldn't mean very much. My upbringing and my faith both encourage me to think of marriage as a holy bond between a man and a woman, broken only by an extreme violation of trust.

Because of my own physical problems, it has been doubly difficult to deal with Betty's illness. My friend Dan Vos, our building contractor, came to visit me recently, just to chat about old times and catch up with one another—it had been a while since I had seen Dan. He now wears two hearing aids, and between his hearing and my difficulty with speaking, it's a wonder we were able to communicate at all. But we pulled our chairs closer together and talked seriously for a while about aging—about our own health, Betty's condition, and Rich's heart problems.

As weak as Betty is, as much as she has changed, God has given me a deeper love for her. Dan sympathized with me, recalling his relationship with his first wife, Ruth, who had tragically died of a brain tumor in 1967. "It's a love we can't explain, isn't it?" he said. "It's something that grows in spite of illness, weakness, or age." Dan was right. Betty is more precious to me now than ever before. In a society overtaken by twisted views of marriage and love, traditional fidelity may seem outdated or useless. But the timeless and self-sacrificing love Betty and I have shared has made both of us happier, more complete people, and has reflected God's continuing work in our lives. For many years, as Rich and I built Amway, Betty willingly sacrificed much for my sake. Now, in her weakness, I have an opportunity to love and serve her in return. Fidelity pays off.

Dan and I talked about all of these things and prayed together briefly. He was a great encouragement to me and had many wise words of advice as one who had come through hardship with a stronger, deeper faith. I asked Dan how he endured his wife's passing. "Jesus Christ has been there long before us," he said. "I had strength given to me long before I even needed it. And when that time comes you'll be able to take it too."

Around the same time that Betty began having the very early stages of Alzheimer's disease, I began to notice a slight loss of manual dexterity. For a year or so, it didn't have a noticeable effect on my life. Betty commented on it once or twice, but neither of us thought much of it. It was the summer of 1988 when I realized that something was definitely not right, and subsequent tests confirmed that I was in the early stages of Parkinson's disease.

We go through life not even thinking about our physical abilities—our brains command our bodies to perform tasks and our bodies obediently comply. When the communication lines stop working properly, it can be a serious handicap. What began with reduced manual dexterity soon extended to difficulties with speech, so I greatly reduced my public-speaking engagements.

I have been very reluctant to accept medical help for my condition. People close to me have approached me several times about various kinds of treatment, but I've usually been resistant. Part of my hesitancy was due to the invasion of my privacy that was sure to come with treatment, and part was simply a distrust of medical care.

Bill Nicholson approached me several times, however, saying I should go see this or that specialist. My children also have expressed their concerns and presented me with plans of their own. Finally, Bill told me, "Jay, this is the last time I'm ever going to try you on this subject, but I'd feel bad if I didn't try once more. There's been a lot of people who tell me that they think you have Parkinson's and there are things they can do to help you. Here's what you can do, if you're willing to do something about it."

Bill had no idea what I would eventually be willing to do about Parkinson's and other diseases.

CHAPTER 20

Enduring Legacy

For years Betty and I have contributed to the work of charities, hospitals, schools, and other worthwhile institutions through the Jay and Betty Van Andel Foundation. It's really more of a family foundation now, because our children have been brought into the decision-making process and are now helping to review contributions from the foundation. In this way the legacy of philanthropy is being taught to the next generation.

The highlight of the foundation is now the Van Andel Institute, a worldwide independent research organization dedicated to preserving, enhancing, and expanding the frontiers of medical science to benefit mankind. It will represent one of the largest private philanthropic activities in medical research history, aiming to achieve a scientific quality comparable to the Howard Hughes Institute and as a source of medical breakthroughs in the twenty-first century. The Van Andel Institute's Board of Scientific Advisors includes over one hundred years of collective scientific experience among its five members.

Some people might wonder why, when I have such great disdain for mainstream medical care, the Van Andel Institute for medical research is such a large part of my estate planning. In my mind, it's not an inconsistency, because while I don't hold traditional methods of medical treatment in particularly high regard, medical research is fascinating to me. The human body is a wondrous creation of God, and learning all we can about it is obviously important. Since my early days with Nutrilite, I've been very interested in how nutrition affects health. The unsurpassed assembly of scientific knowledge at the Van Andel Institute should yield real progress in medical science, with important implications for heart disease, cancer, and cognitive and nervous-system diseases like Alzheimer's and Parkinson's.

Currently, there is no definite cure or treatment for Alzheimer's disease. Scientists do not yet know what causes Alzheimer's, though researchers are investigating possible causes for the neurological damage, like viruses, chemical deficiencies, environmental toxins, immune system deficiencies, and genetic abnormalities. The disease, which is the fourth leading killer of adults in the United States, afflicts about five million Americans and brings grief and pain and loss to friends and family members. Approximately 10 percent of Americans over sixty-five have what is probably Alzheimer's, and for those over eighty-five, the percentage rises even more. It develops gradually, causing the victim to lose intellectual capacity and become confused and disoriented. At first, the only signs may be an increased difficulty finding words or finishing thoughts. Friends and relatives may begin to notice memory loss, impaired judgment, and a change in personality. Some forgetfulness is part of the normal aging process, but the atrophying of the brain associated with Alzheimer's disease may eventually cause its victims to become lost in familiar surroundings, forget names of close relatives, lose the ability to read or write, and forget how to tell time or use a key. Many become incapable of taking care of themselves and often require twenty-four-hour care and supervision.

Parkinson's disease, unlike Alzheimer's disease, is a motor-system disorder. While cognitive diseases such as Alzheimer's reduce the victim's ability to think or remember, motor-system disorders affect movement or speech. Parkinson's disease can cause stiffness, shaking or trembling, slowness of movement, and impaired coordination and balance. Diagnosis of Parkinson's is difficult, but estimates show that more than half a million Americans are afflicted with the disease. Pope John Paul, Billy Graham, Attorney General Janet Reno, and Johnny Cash are reported to have it. Scientists have found that Parkinson's is caused by a loss of certain cells in a part of the brain associated with muscle activity, but the reason for this cell death is as yet unknown. A relatively new theory proposes that some Parkinson's victims may have a genetic predisposition to the disease. Treatment commonly includes medication and may involve surgery in rare cases.

As I entertained thoughts about the potential for medical progress, I realized that our family had a unique opportunity to pass on a legacy to all humanity that few envision and even fewer can afford. I entrusted the realization of the most important part of my legacy to my youngest son, Dave, and to Dr. Luis Tomatis.

Dave, who serves as chairman of the Van Andel Institute, is guiding its operation and overseeing the construction of the impressive new building. While all of my children have had some input, Dave has been especially charged with seeing that my intentions for the institute are carried out. By keeping members of the Van Andel family closely involved, the institute is kept as near as possible to my purpose in founding the institute.

My friend, Luis Tomatis, M.D., a former thoracic and cardiovascular surgeon, laid the foundation for the Van Andel Institute as president. After retiring in 1995 from a distinguished career as a heart surgeon at Butterworth Hospital here in Grand Rapids, Dr. Tomatis devoted his time to developing the institute. He consulted 146 experienced researchers from the United States and sixteen foreign countries, visited a dozen similar research facilities, and laid out the organizational form of the institute. In the summer of 1996, Dr. Tomatis convened sixteen scientists in Grand Rapids as informal advisors to the fledgling institute. This group gave the institute its first direction, advising us to pursue molecular biology and genetics as our first avenue of research. Six months later, Dr. Tomatis had gathered together a world-class Board of Scientific Advisors that would secure the scientific quality of the institute's research.

The board consists of brilliant, visionary individuals recognized by their peers as top in their fields. Among those contacted was Michael Brown, M.D., from the University of Texas Medical Center at Dallas, who, in association with Joseph Goldstein, M.D., won the Nobel Prize in medicine in 1988 for their work in the metabolism of cholesterol. Once he became thoroughly convinced that we were determined to create an institute that would eventually be among the best in the world, he turned his inexhaustible energies as chairman of the Board of Scientific Advisors to enroll his partner of twenty-five years and co–Nobel laureate Joseph Goldstein, M.D., of the University of Texas Medical Center, Southwestern Medical Center at Dallas. Also brought on board were Richard Axel, M.D., of Columbia University; Daniel Nathans, M.D., of the

Johns Hopkins University School of Medicine; and Phillip A. Sharp, Ph.D., of the Massachusetts Institute of Technology. The last two, also Nobel laureates, help form an impressive think tank. They are charged to select, within the next five years, the other areas of scientific research for the Van Andel Research Institute and help us get the Grand Rapids campus under way.

The excitement we all felt as our plans began to take shape was contagious. At the December 1996 press conference announcing the appointment of these scientists, Dr. Michael Brown remarked:

> [W]e are present at the birth of something that will live long after all of us. . . . We hope to create an institute that will apply the strongest aspects of basic science directly to the prevention and cure of human disease. It's very rare that any enterprise of this scope has ever begun. This is not an everyday occurrence on a national scale or a worldwide scale. This is as big an event for the world as it is for Grand Rapids, because we think that this institute has the capacity in its final form to be the leading institute of medical research in the world.

This Board of Scientific Advisors immediately began to focus on some promising avenues of research. There are many well-funded disease-oriented research efforts, but they believe that science should now study the basic mechanisms of cell function. We need to know how cells and tissues normally function, and why they cease to function or act in such an abnormal way that they produce disease and death.

Previous research has already laid the groundwork for what our board proposes to do. As scientists began to study basic cell mechanisms, they found out that apparently dissimilar afflictions like hardening of the arteries (atherosclerosis),

Alzheimer's, and arthritis may have the common factor of chronic inflammation. And retinitis pigmentosa, a very common cause of blindness in the elderly, could hold one of the answers to our questions about cancer. Retinitis pigmentosa is caused by the overgrowth of microscopic blood vessels (capillaries) at the end of the nerve that transmits the images from the eye to the brain. In cancer patients, the only capillaries that grow are in the tumor tissue. If we can find out how these tiny vessels are stimulated to grow, we may also find the way to stop them from growing. We could starve to death the cancer that depends on them to get nutrition. Normal tissues would remain unaffected. The reverse mechanism could be used to stimulate the growth of small vessels in order to avoid or limit the damage of heart attacks.

The medical research center will begin its operations with a program dedicated to molecular and genetic basic science and to clinical research. The ultimate goal will be human disease prevention and treatment. Dr. Brown and the other scientists on the board of advisors believe that by better understanding each individual's unique genetic makeup, specific recommendations can be made to avoid health problems later in life. Dr. Brown explains the hope the institute offers:

> What we see ahead of us is a world in which people can tailor their environment to match what their genes demand, so that if you discover that you have a particularly high risk of a particular kind of cancer, for example, based on your genetic makeup, you can take the right combination of nutrients or vitamins that will act for you to prevent that disease. . . . In the past we've had to have a one-size-fits-all set of recommendations for everybody. For instance, we recommend that everybody be on a low-fat diet, even though doctors know that two-thirds of people don't need a low-fat diet. The problem is that we don't know how to

identify that two-thirds. . . . Each of us is a biochemical individual, and modern molecular biology and genetics has taught us how to analyze the genes of each person in order to figure out what is the most optimal for them. We can't do it with any completeness today, but maybe in the next twenty years, with the Van Andel Institute, we can start to achieve some of that.

As a first step, the institute will seek out the best brains in medical research to work in a state-of-the-art, well-funded headquarters facility. Then the institute will branch to other campuses dedicated to other research problems, locating wherever the best scientists and support facilities are located.

Research into the causes and potential cures for Alzheimer's, Parkinson's, and other diseases is promising but requires much more support. As the demographics of the United States change to include a larger proportion of elderly people, I expect that Americans will be willing to fund efforts to reduce the terrible effects of these diseases. I hope that my own contributions to medical research will be followed by increased support from other entrepreneurs, charitable foundations, and concerned individuals.

The organization and private funding of the Van Andel Institute's research will make it uniquely effective. Whereas much medical research today is made less effective by the continual, energy-consuming search for federal grants, the Van Andel Institute will be able to undertake high-risk, comprehensive research without enslaving itself to that continuous waste of their time and minds. Rather than funneling resources to lobbying efforts or wasting them on commonplace research, Van Andel Institute funds will flow directly to its frontier research.

My hope is that the research done at the Van Andel Institute will be truly pathbreaking. The focus will be on those questions about human health that are passed over by traditional research institutions—those areas that are underresearched and underfunded because of the outcome uncertainty involved. The advantages for us are, first, that we are not duplicating efforts, and second, by pushing out the frontiers of science, we could reap significant rewards missed by other institutions. Because the private funding of the institute allows it to take a long-term view, researchers are free to pursue a promising line of research even if it doesn't end in a breakthrough. Solid, well-planned science that stops short of a breakthrough is still good science that may help others down the road to a great discovery.

Realizing that the Van Andel Institute would create employment and trigger economic growth wherever it is located, I directed that Grand Rapids be the permanent home of the Van Andel Institute headquarters. Furthermore, to help revitalize the city's core, I asked that the building be constructed downtown. Besides its encouragement of local business, the structure will represent a friendly attitude toward hospitals, universities, and the whole community. We will open its auditorium and public spaces to the social, religious, intellectual, and artistic forces that shape the city.

I envision a living institution that gives summer employment to high school students to motivate them in scientific paths in a superb learning environment. I envision our scientists at all levels becoming involved with the local schools and colleges, and local science teachers getting further continuous updates in our institute. I envision scientists from all over the world coming to work in our institute, and I envision national and international congresses held in my native town, drawn by a leading medical research center. And I envision the Lord's hand shaping this, our legacy.

Consistent with the quality of all the aspects of the institute we engaged Rafael Vinoly, the visionary architect who designed the Tokyo International Forum, a 1.4-million-square-foot structure that has become that city's trademark. Vinoly has several massive projects in different stages of realization: a $150 million courthouse for the city of New York, a thirty-thousand-seat stadium for Princeton University, and research institutes for Columbia University and Professor Montaignier of the City University of New York (who discovered the AIDS virus). We were impressed by his insatiable curiosity, creative ingenuity, and attention to detail. Vinoly has designed a beautiful, state-of-the-art laboratory for us. It will be built in two phases. The first phase, a one-hundred-thousand-square-foot building, began in February 1998 with a scheduled completion date at the end of 1999. It is our hope that the millennium will find us up and running.

In May 1998, the Van Andel Research Institute recruited a very talented researcher and organizer, George Vande Woude, Ph.D., as its first research director.

Dr. Vande Woude is an internationally recognized expert in molecular oncology (the study of cell component behavior in cancer.) He comes from the National Cancer Institute (NCI) in Bethesda, Maryland, where he is developing strategies to reorganize their intramural research. This division, the largest basic science research enterprise in the world, is composed of 32 laboratories and more than 180 senior researchers dedicated to understanding the mechanisms of the cell function that can ultimately be used to produce new cancer treatments. A graduate of Rutgers University, Dr. Vande Woude received many honors and awards including election to the National Academy of Sciences.

I'm confident that he is the appropriate person to lead the scientific efforts of our institute.

LOVE GROWS DEEPER

Part of my intense interest in medical research and the Van Andel Institute stems from my concern over Betty's Alzheimer's disease, Rich's recurrent heart problems, and my own recent battles with physiological problems. I know what it is like to see loved ones suffer from the failings of the human body and to witness their recovery under the care of skillful physicians. Through the Van Andel Institute, I have hope that the material blessings that God has bestowed upon me during my life can be used to reduce human suffering and extend lives.

In June of 1997 Rich underwent heart transplant surgery. Many years of cardiovascular problems had left Rich's heart permanently damaged, and the risky surgery was necessary to give Rich more years of precious life. The long, agonizing months of waiting for a heart were finally rewarded, and Rich made dramatic progress in the weeks after the surgery. I am convinced that his optimism and strong faith, and the prayers of thousands of caring people, carried Rich through this very difficult time.

Though Rich was in London for the surgery, we kept in close contact during the wait for the heart and the recovery. As we talked, I found that the decades have strengthened the unique friendship that Rich and I have. God has had his hand on both our lives, and he has blessed that friendship in a way that very few other people can understand. For more than half a century, we have experienced good times and bad times together, and all of it has worked out to the glory of God. As health problems afflict both of us, it strikes me that God has given us human friendship to remind us of his continuous presence with us in times of trouble.

CHAPTER 21

The Anchors
of Life

Large boats and ships, when a storm threatens, will sail to the leeward, or wind-sheltered, side of an island and secure themselves with two or more anchors. If the anchors hold, the ship will not be blown away or capsized by the winds and waves. Poorly placed anchors, or weak anchor chains, can jeopardize the safety of all aboard.

Everyone must choose several parts of life that can hold one fast when troubles come. These "anchors" must be trustworthy and reliable, so that they do not fail when they are most needed. There have been three anchors to my life—moorings that have held me secure and steadfast while the world raged around me. These are my faith, my family, and my friends.

My religious faith has been my most trusted anchor. It has been my mainstay and comfort throughout my life. In the tradition of my Dutch ancestors, there can be no substitute for a deep-felt reliance upon God for help and sustenance. Armed with the faith my parents taught me, I always had a bright star to guide me and the kind, loving hand of the Lord to hold me. His strength inspired and consoled me in the darkest hours. I have never been alone in my life, for He has been with me.

My family has been my strongest anchor and greatest treasure. Nothing in life has been more precious to me than my marriage to Betty and the wonderful times we have spent together through the decades. My Dutch character has given me a restraint on outward manifestation of feelings, but while I may have portrayed an image of aloofness, in reality I have given and received in return very much love. Since the day I met Betty I have loved her without pause, and I thank God for allowing me the privilege to keep doing so.

My children have grown to reflect their mother's dedication and our love. They are on the way to fulfill their own destinies in their own special and different ways, and I watch them with great pride.

About twenty years ago we hired as steward of the *Enterprise* a young Cuban man who through the years became the favorite of both families when we were on board. Francisco (Frank) Padron spoiled all of us with his attention, refined manners, and loyalty. We both trusted and liked him very much. Therefore, it made sense that I retained him recently as my personal assistant, and he has made the transition from good health to struggling with Parkinson's so much easier for me. His cheerful face is the last I see every night and the first to greet me every morning. His companionship and support are very important in my daily life.

My friends have been my bow anchor—they keep me pointed into the wind so that I don't give up when it seems that life's troubles could sink me. There are many people to whom I owe so much of who I am, who have helped me to enjoy life even when its tempests are fiercest. Any listing of those dear friends could not come close to being complete, but I would be thoughtless not to make special mention of my longest and best friend and business partner, Rich DeVos.

In so many ways Rich has been a part of my family, and I a part of his. It is astounding what God has done in both of us since we first became friends nearly six decades ago. Rich and I have not only complemented each other but become who we are because of our friendship and association. Others who have enjoyed a close, lifelong bond of friendship will understand me best. I don't have a recipe for such a friendship, but when you find "that friend," you will know it.

Each of these three anchors has helped me weather the storms of life. God has been truly good to me to give me faith in him, to bless me with such a wonderful family, and to strengthen me with good friends.

For seventy-four years now God has blessed me with life and breath. He has given me the freedom to try, to fail, and to try again and again. After many trials he blessed me with success. It is my duty and great privilege to share that success with others. Through the Amway business and my own giving through the years, I have enjoyed witnessing positive changes in human lives. Today, throughout the world, three million people are experiencing the freedom and fulfillment of building their own businesses through Amway. Many are discovering that entrepreneurship can be more rewarding than anything else they are capable of doing. Some have left careers as physicians, attorneys, and corporate executives to develop their distributorships full-time. Others, frustrated by the barriers to raising capital to start a business, have found that Amway provides a low-cost gateway into the world of self-employment. And millions are learning management skills, "people" skills, and self-confidence along the way.

The opportunities presented by Amway have been the clear outgrowth of the beliefs Rich and I both have in free enterprise, liberty, and political freedom. Through Amway, distributors serve as "ambassadors of entrepreneurship" throughout the world. As a result, citizens of eighty countries are sharing the benefits of the free-enterprise system today. And they are sharing the hope of a better life.

THE HOPE OF ENTREPRENEURSHIP

Half a century ago, when Rich and I were running our airplane business, we never imagined what would grow out of our partnership. Looking back, I recall all the fun we had and the important lessons we learned. We discovered the value of persistence in the face of discouragement. We learned about balancing business and family obligations and about the importance of morality in the entrepreneur's life. We learned to work hard and dream big.

Each stage of development of Nutrilite and then Amway taught us something new. Nutrilite's early successes gave us experience in direct selling and the foundation for the Amway Sales and Marketing Plan. Their later errors in management taught us the importance of faithfulness in business dealings and the necessity of maintaining good distributor relations. The first years of Amway taught us how to build a first-class manufacturing facility and guide its rapid growth. Bruising legal battles and media attacks from the late 1970s to the mid-1980s taught us the importance of good lines of communication with government and the public. The positive impact Amway's dollars made on the Grand Rapids area and all over the world demonstrated to us the necessity of corporate citizenship.

Some of these lessons were learned the hard way, but each one of them helped make Amway stronger. Amway has evolved to the point where its extensive distributor network is a potent force in American and international marketing. Many companies will now engineer product ideas and sales campaigns around using Amway's distributors as a model for the marketing organization. Amway is much more than a soap company now—the myriad of products and services Amway markets have gained the loyalty of customers and the respect of the competition.

Amway is destined to be far, far greater than it is today, because the chance for personal improvement and independence that the Amway Plan offers has universal appeal. Amway holds out the opportunity to fulfill a dream that's common to people of all nations, all races, all age groups, all cultures, and all professions. If that opportunity can be offered in the same form, and if customers continue to be excited about our products, Amway will continue to grow.

Entrepreneurship is not dead, despite many severe limitations on the freedom of business to do its job. Amway's success proves that millions of entrepreneurs are very much alive and involved in the wealth-creation process. Entrepreneurs are doing their part in the economy—growing their businesses, funding education, art, and research, supporting their churches and local charities, and enhancing the quality of life for everyone. In every country, under every economic system, these men and women are struggling to create a better life for themselves and everyone around them. Sometimes the government works with and for entrepreneurs; sometimes it places barriers in their path. But no matter what government may do to hinder their essential work, entrepreneurs will always be there. And as long as entrepreneurs are with us, and they live moral lives, there is hope.

THE HOPE OF HEALING

For me, one of the greatest joys in building a successful business is the opportunity to share newly created wealth with others. Rich and I both have done this in our own ways, and our children also know the importance of generosity. My own priority in giving has been to expand the hope of healing.

The Van Andel Institute's medical research and education will return manyfold to humanity what society has so abundantly given us. I can think of no better way to touch the lives of each person on earth than to support the research that will extend human life and reduce human pain and suffering. It is not a desire for fame or public accolades that has propelled me into founding the Van Andel Institute. My motivation is rooted, first, in my personal experiences with crippling and life-threatening diseases. When you have felt the desperation and helplessness of watching a loved one suffer from a long illness, you have known the hope that comes from knowing that research progress is being made. Thankfully, adjustments in my medication have given me improvements recently, allowing me to take on some limited speaking engagements and function more normally. Second, I am under obligation to make the best possible use of the resources that have been entrusted to me by God. Fighting illness and death, which are the results of the first sin in the Garden of Eden, is to me a worthy goal. Perhaps, also, people will associate my name with the institute and recall that the fruits of capitalism made this invaluable research possible. If they do, then I have conveyed a message more powerfully and permanently than in all my speeches on free enterprise.

In God's grand design of the universe, I am just one more person. The Creator, in his wisdom, gives each of us diverse talents that he delights to see us use to his glory. To me, for a reason yet unknown, he has given the opportunity to spread his message of faith, freedom, and hope to the many people that Rich and I have encountered in our business, public, and private lives. I fervently hope that their lives are a little better because of that encounter.

Jay Van Andel, the Co-founder of Amway Corporation, was born on June 3, 1924 in Grand Rapids, Michigan. He is a graduate of Grand Rapids Christian High School and attended Calvin College in Grand Rapids, Morningside College in Sioux City, Iowa, Pratt Business School in Pratt, Kansas, and Yale University Aviation Cadet School in New Haven, Connecticut.

In August of 1952 he married the former Betty Hoekstra. They have four children, Nan, Steven, Barbara and David. Jay and Betty's sense of family, first demonstrated in the upbringing of their children, transcended traditional bounds, finding its way into relationships formed both in business, neighbors, the community of Grand Rapids and beyond.

Years of dedication reflect Jay Van Andel's tremendous personal energy—energy brought to many and varied interests, not the least of which is the Amway Corporation. Amway is one of the largest direct selling companies. The Company offers more than 450 Amway-name products, thousands of brand-name items through the PERSONAL SHOPPERS catalog, plus a variety of services and education products. These products are sold by more than 3 million entrepreneurs operating in 46 affiliate markets. A phenomenal success story of the American entrepreneurial spirit, Amway was founded in 1959 by Jay Van Andel and Richard DeVos. Its unheralded growth in the decades that followed has been a source of inspiration and amelioration for literally millions around the world.

As Amway's presence reached around the world so did Jay Van Andel's reputation. In 1992, President George Bush appointed Jay to serve as the United States Ambassador and Commissioner General to Genoa Expo '92. He has also served as Chairman of the U.S. Chamber of Commerce, Director of the Gerald R. Ford Foundation, Chairman of the Netherlands-American Bicentennial Commission, and as a member of the U.S.O. World Board of Governors. He is a Trustee of the Jamestown Foundation, Hudson Institute and the Heritage Foundation, as well as the Founder of the Van Andel Institute for Education and Medical Research in Grand Rapids.

AWARDS AND HONORS

Religious Heritage of America, Business and Professional Leader of the Year Award—1974, Great Living American Award—1982.

Honorary Doctorates from Northern Michigan University—1976, Ferris State University—1978, Western Michigan University—1980, Grand Valley State University—1992, Michigan State University—1997.

Golden Plate Award, American Academy of Achievement—1981.

Direct Selling Association Hall of Fame—1987.

Greater Grand Rapids Business Hall of Fame—1989.

United Nations Environment Programme Achievement Award, recipient on behalf of Amway—1989.

Business Person of the Year, Economic Club of Grand Rapids—1990.

Sales & Marketing Executives International Academy of Achievement, Charter Inductee—1990.

Adam Smith Free Enterprise Award, from the American Legislative Exchange Council—1993.

Edison Award, American Marketing Association—1994.

Clare Boothe Luce Award, from the Heritage Foundation—1998.

George Washington Honor Medal, Freedoms Foundation.

Gold Medals, Netherlands Societies of New York and Philadelphia.

Member, MENSA Society of the U.S.A.

Patron Award, Michigan Foundation for the Arts.

Knighted, Grand Officer, Order of Orange Nassau-Netherlands.

Honorary Member, Omicron Delta Kappa National Honors Society.